Studio Bass Masters

*Session Tips & Techniques
from Top Bass Players*

by Keith Rosiér

Miller
Freeman
Books

San Francisco

Published by Miller Freeman Books
600 Harrison Street, San Francisco, CA 94107
Publishers of *Keyboard, Bass Player,* and *Guitar Player* magazines

 Miller Freeman
A United News & Media publication

Distributed to the book trade in the U.S. and Canada by
Publishers Group West, P.O. Box 8843, Emeryville, CA 94662

Distributed to the music trade in the U.S. and Canada by
Hal Leonard Publishing, P.O. Box 13819, Milwaukee, WI 53213

Editor: Richard Johnston
Cover design: Sandra Kelch
Design and typesetting: Greene Design
Original art, layout, and design: Doug Johnson—Airplay
        Graphics, Garden Grove, CA.
Original music transcriptions/tab: Dan Hughart
Music editor: Jesse Gress

Produced by Keith Rosiér
for LittleBun Productions

Library of Congress Cataloging in Publication Data:
Rosiér, Keith.
        Studio bass masters : a survival guide for the modern studio bassist /
        by Keith Rosiér.
        p. cm.
ISBN 0-87930-558-4
1. Bass guitar—Instruction and study. 2. Double bass—Instruction and study.
3. Sound studios. 4. Bass guitarists—Interviews. 5. Double bassists—
Interviews. I. Title.
MT599.B4R675 1999
787.87'023—dc21   98-41677
                                              CIP
                                               MN

Printed in the United States of America
99 00 01 02 03 04   5 4 3 2 1

Cover photo by Paul Haggard

For Madeleine, Denise, and Mom

Acknowledgments

My sincere thanks to: Nathan East, Larry Paxton, Don Was, Neil Stubenhaus, Bob Wray, Lee Sklar, Dave Pomeroy, Mike Brignardello, Glenn Worf, Mike Chapman, Hutch Hutchinson, Roy Huskey Jr., Bob Moore, Pete Anderson, and Dusty Wakeman.

To my wife, Denise and my daughter, Madeleine—Thanks for your love and support.

To Doug Johnson—Your artistic touch and suggestions were invaluable to this project.

To Dan Hughart—Thanks for the excellent transcriptions.

To Hutch—Thanks for helping me get started by being the first interview.

To Matt Kelsey—Thank you for your kindness, and for believing in this project. My family and I appreciate your care with all aspects of this book.

To Jan Hughes—Thanks for all your help, and patience with a project that had many twists and changes.

To Richard Johnston—Thanks RJ. Your belief and kind words were invaluable—our best to Trisha.

To the staff of Miller Freeman Books—I love the book, and it's been a pleasure working with such a class act.

To Jeff Schroedl—Thanks for all the suggestions.

Additional thanks to: Marcel East, *Bass Player* magazine, Kittra, Rebecca A. Wolk, Garth Brooks, Tatsuo Kusumoto, Fourplay, Gregory Isola, Bonnie Raitt, Lisa Thomas, Quincy Jones, Harrie, Richard Newman, Russell Jones, Little Bun, Dewayne Blackwell, John Carruthers, LaBella, Richard Cocco Jr., Earl Bud Lee, Denise Dumke, Studio One, Dangerous Waters Music recording studio, Pro Tools, Gloria at LaBella, Dee Dee Hart, Adrian Mueller, Alison Stubenhaus, Benny Golson, Queen Latifah, Judith Bright, Gisela Klose, Robert Johnson, Michael Henderson, and Barefoot Servants.

Table of Contents

Foreword

Neurological researchers at Cal Tech and Washington University in St. Louis have made incredible discoveries over the last decade regarding musical connectivity in the developing brain. These doctors have isolated three interrelated areas in the tempora section of the ventricular system. The first relates to the synaptic connections that govern our processing of low musical frequencies. The second involves our ability to comprehend rhythm. Curiously, the third concerns the positional identity of patterns inherent in the "cooing" sounds mothers make to communicate with newborn infants. Babies with extra encoding receptors in one of these areas tend to possess accelerated expression patterns in the other two. What this suggests, at least to professor David B. Clifford at Washington University, is that those brains with deeper capabilities for understanding mothers, love and, subsequently, in possession of greater self-confidence and inner security, will also display a predilection for playing the bass.

While, I'm sure, this theory will be the subject of intense debate, it will probably have great resonance for the musicians featured in this fine collection. As the research confirms, bass is not an instrument for ego-starved hotshots who clamor for all the attention a spotlight can offer. It is, in fact, the domain of supportive, generous souls, who derive joy and satisfaction by providing a solid, musical foundation. These stalwart troops stand unperturbed as megalomaniacal frontmen and pyrotechnical soloists step over them like dogs—oftentimes reaping financial rewards and personal fame dwarfing that of their low-frequency compatriots.

The studio masters profiled in this book are all individuals whom I have admired for a long time. In some cases, they are good friends who've helped me in the studio on numerous recordings. They never cease to amaze me with their boundless talent for infusing fresh, creative ideas into each song and for providing the infectious pulse that stands as a beacon of inspiration for all the other musicians on the session. They are, however, much more than groove messengers; these bassists must continually be at the top of their harmonic game—a simple, well-placed passing tone can create an inversion that breaks your heart and enables a record to emotionally flourish (see Brian Wilson, Willie Dixon). The highest compliment that I can pay these bassists is that I regularly hire them to work on sessions that I would kill to play on. I do so without resentment or jealousy because I always love to hear them play and they contribute so much to the success of each record.

One last thing, however: I made up all that neurological crap in paragraph one. In reality, people pick up the bass because it's an easy instrument to fake your way on, there are fewer bassists than guitar players—making gigs more plentiful—and because nobody in the audience notices when you make a really big mistake. A keen understanding of those simple facts will prove to be invaluable in the pages to come as you attempt to separate truth from malarkey.

—Don Was

Introduction

Master: A person preeminent in a discipline, as in art or science.

Playing on a record (master) session is the dream of many bassists, but just a select few are able to make a living this way. These bassists are not just lucky; they worked hard developing their technique and spent many years gaining the experience necessary to survive in the highly competitive session world.

Studio Bass Masters will introduce you to some of today's top recording bassists, exploring their styles and approaches through their words and bass lines. We'll also examine the styles and reading skills required for any bassist interested in a session career, and we'll find out what a Grammy-winning producer and a top recording engineer expect from bassists.

Studio Bass Masters is dedicated to the great bassists of the past and present whose playing defined the role of session bass and who inspire us to become better players—musicians such as Bob Moore, Chuck Domanico, Ray Brown, Joe Osborn, Chuck Rainey, Ray Pohlman, Tommy Cogbill, Ron Carter, Duck Dunn, Willie Dixon, Carol Kaye, and James Jamerson. Besides these artists and the other players featured in this book, you should check out recordings by bassists such as Abraham Laboriel, Will Lee, Bob Glaub, Tony Levin, Willie Weeks, and David Hungate. This book is dedicated as well to the late Leo Fender, who gave recording bassists the definitive tool of their craft. I hope that by studying this book you will someday become a studio bass master.

Keith Rosier

The Recording Process

Recording studios come in all shapes and sizes. They can be found in garages, homes, and specially-built facilities, and even in trucks for mobile recording.

Most major-label artists' tracking dates take place at professional studios that can accommodate bands and sometimes full orchestras. The usual format is 2-inch magnetic tape recorded on a 24-track machine by companies such as Studer, MCI, and Ampex. Some studios also use digital tape machines by such companies as Sony, Tascam (the DA-88), and Alesis (ADAT).

Instruments and microphones usually feed into a 24-channel mixing console that has mike preamps at each channel's input for adjusting the recording level of the bass, guitar, vocal mike, and other sources. The mixing console's outputs are connected to the tape machine.

MIXING

After recording is finished, mixing begins. The output of the 2-inch 24-track or digital tape machine is fed back into the mixing console, where individual levels are adjusted, EQ and effects are added, and the tracks are combined and balanced to the satisfaction of the producer, artist, and engineer. The mixing console's stereo outputs are then fed into a 2-track tape recorder or 2-track DAT (digital) recorder. This 2-track final mix is taken to a mastering engineer.

MASTERING

The mastering engineer plays the final mix in a very accurate sonic environment that allows the producer to hear problems such as an overly loud instrument or too much treble or bass. Mastering engineers can adjust their systems to boost or cut bass or treble and even lower specific frequencies' output. They can also compress certain instruments or the whole mix slightly to bring up other instruments around, for instance, a drum track that's too loud. The 2-track final mix is plugged into the mastering console, adjusted, and the output recorded onto a 2-track format called the CD master. This is sent to the CD or record plant for duplication.

THE TOOLS

Direct box (DI). This allows for proper connection between your bass and the recording console. A DI contains a transformer that converts the bass signal to the proper impedance and "balances" the output for connection to the console. The output of most DIs is XLR balanced, which allows for long cable runs with less noise and little frequency loss; most consoles are set up for XLR input. Without a DI the high end of your bass can be affected, making it sound dull

Mike preamp. A typical instrument's output level is not high enough to allow a tape machine to record it properly. To solve this problem most recording consoles have a mike preamp built into the input of each channel. The mike pre's level control allows the balanced, impedance-matched signal from your DI to be boosted to the +4dB most pro-grade tape machines require.

Some engineers like to bypass the mixing console and connect outboard tube mike preamps directly to the tape machine's inputs. This allows for the purest recording of an instrument. In this configuration the chain would be bass guitar to DI, DI to mike pre, mike pre to tape machine. The proper recording level is achieved by adjusting the mike pre's level control.

Equalization (EQ). Most recording consoles feature an EQ section for each channel to adjust bass, midrange, and treble. Pro-grade consoles feature parametric EQ, which lets you boost or cut specific frequency points. EQ is not normally used until mixdown, because a sound chosen when tracking might not work for the final mix.

Compression/limiting. Compression reduces a signal's dynamic range, attenuating loud notes and making quieter notes more audible. When set properly, compression can make a bass track even and punchy across the frequency spectrum, which makes mixing easier. You shouldn't rely on compression to smooth out your technique, however; most session bassists use minimal compression because they play with a consistent attack.

Most compressors have attack, release, and ratio functions. For bass a slower attack setting allows your natural attack to come through, and a slower release helps make the compression less noticeable. Ratio determines the overall amount of compression, with the higher settings creating a more obvious effect. When using compression, the unaffected signal should be A/B'd with the altered signal to make sure compression is being used properly.

The compressor can be put right after the DI, though some engineers prefer it last in the signal chain. This lets the compressor smooth out peaks the EQ settings create.

Limiting is used to attenuate only a signal's peaks, like those produced when you pop or slap a bass. A number of amps feature limiters to reduce the distortion peaks can cause. If set improperly, though, limiting can give your bass an unnatural squashed sound.

TWO

The Sessions

Demo Sessions

Most of the session players we look up to started out playing on demos. A demo (demon-stration) tape displays a song or an artist and is the most common way for established artists to audition to new songs. Demos sessions are also a good way for bassists to learn about the recording process. In cities such as Los Angeles and Nashville there are demo sessions for songwriters who have deals with publishers, for up-and-coming artists looking for a deal, and for local bands looking to make a CD. Demos can be informal. Many are recorded in homes, and you might be the only musician present while you overdub a bass part. The hallmark of demos is speed: The goal of a typical Nashville songwriter session is to record five songs in three hours. Learning to quickly deliver winning bass lines makes the transition to master sessions go more smoothly. You can also make valuable contacts in demo sessions. Mike Chapman played on Garth Brooks' demos, and when Brooks got a record deal he asked his producer to hire Mike for the master sessions.

SETTING UP

When you walk into the studio, the engineer or producer will probably tell you where to set up in the control room or in the tracking room, or you may have to ask. When you find your spot, take your instruments out of their cases so they can adjust to room temperature.

The engineer usually sets drum sounds first and then moves on to the bass. There will almost always be a DI for you to plug into. The engineer will ask you to play—always keep your volume control wide open—and will set the level of your bass.

Headphone levels are usually set during the first band run-through. Everyone waits their turn to tell the engineer what they need adjusted in their phones. Some-times everyone is on the same mix, so you might have to compromise and listen to your bass at a lower level than you might prefer.

LEARNING THE TUNE

The artist or producer will pass out charts or expect you to write your own as a demo of the song is played, either on tape or on piano or guitar. Even if the song is simple, you should always make a chart. As recording progresses the arrangement can change drastically; I've seen players hold up sessions because they couldn't keep track of all the changes by memory. This could have been avoided if they had marked down the changes on a chart.

TRACKING THE SONG

You are hired to play exactly what the artist or producer asks you to play to the best of your ability—no exceptions. Keep a smile on your face and try to add a good creative vibe to the session. Don't make judgments about a song's quality. If your bass part is the only good thing about the track, so be it. Successful session players present a positive, professional attitude and never forget they're hired to play their very best at all times.

Some producers and artists expect players to come up with arrangement ideas if needed, while some might not want to hear anything from you besides the part you're asked to play. It's up to you to gauge the situation and respond accordingly.

There are times the artist won't like what you've played and will ask you to come up with something else. If you are easily insulted by this kind of situation, you should be in another line of work. Artists want session players who are willing to work with them and who have no problem with being told their part isn't working. Copping an attitude on a session is a good way to stop your phone from ringing.

You're hired to use your musical and technical expertise to help a song reach its full artistic and commercial potential, but don't think every song requires you to play virtuoso bass lines. Some songs call for the simplest of lines, while others might require a more complex approach—every song and session is different. Bring a fresh outlook to each situation, always making the song your No. 1 priority. As you do more sessions you will learn to hone and trust your intuition. This will help you adjust appropriately to every situation, making everyone happy and you a very popular bassist.

The way you feel can affect your performance. Don't do things that will alter your judgment, like getting wired on coffee or trying to mellow out with a few beers. Such self-medication is likely to make you rush or drag, making it harder for you to create a good feel.

Some producers take three hours on a song—less if it's a demo session—while others might take a day. Whatever happens, be prepared to learn the song quickly and get it down in the first few takes. However, don't fall into the trap of thinking the track you just recorded can't be duplicated or improved. You need the confidence and ability to record the track 25 times if necessary. Be prepared to deliver a winning part over and over again; in other words, until the producer is happy.

PUNCHING IN

If you make a mistake while recording, don't stop playing. Quickly recover and finish the track. You can almost always fix your mistake later by punching in, which is a method of recording over a specific point in the track.

After you've 'fessed up to a mistake, the engineer will find the spot and then start rolling the tape from a few moments before the clinker occurred. At the mistake point the engineer quickly puts your track into record mode so you can lay down the fixer. After you've played the right note or phrase he'll just as quickly take you out of record mode. When punching in, the original and new parts should match exactly in volume and tone, so be sure to set your controls the same and play with an identical attack.

OVERDUBBING

Sometimes you may be asked to play a part for a song that's already recorded. You'll usually do this in the control room with the engineer. You can listen to yourself over the control-room monitors, but you may want to use headphones so you can hear yourself better and be less distracted. The monitors or headphones should be set so you can hear the drums and vocalist well.

It can be harder to groove in an overdub session, since you're not working directly with the drummer. To overcome this, ask the engineer to turn your bass down so you can hear the drums and the rest of the track better.

The Gear

The right equipment makes any job go more smoothly. There are many opinions about which gear is best, but certain products seem to be used on a majority of sessions. Use this section as a starting point and make your own decisions by trying out as much gear as you can to see what works best for you.

Questions you should ask the producer or artist before you show up at a session:
- What kind of date is it—what style of music?
- Do they want fretless, upright, fretted, or all of the above?
- Do they want an amp?

What you need to bring to every session:
- At least two basses—you should always have a backup.
- Two high-quality instrument cables.
- Extra batteries. I recommend Duracells.
- A high-quality tuner with new batteries. Some tuners' pitch will change as batteries wear out. If there is a piano in the studio, check a few of its notes against your tuner; you need to be in tune with the piano if it's used.
- Pen and paper.
- Extra strings and picks.
- Adjustment tools.

THE BASS GUITAR

The Fender Precision Bass and Jazz Bass are the accepted standards for recording electric bass; you can't go wrong if you bring one to a session.

Some bassists try to acquire late '50s to late '60s Fenders because they have a sound seemingly unattainable by later Fender basses. Players attribute this to the amount of music played with the instrument, the wood used, the production methods, and the electronics available during the early pre-CBS era. (CBS owned Fender from 1965 to 1985.) "Age slightly 'softens' the pickups' magnetism," says Venice, California, luthier John Carruthers. "This plus the aging of the wood enhances these instruments' mellow, musical character."

Nonetheless, you don't have to own a vintage Fender to get classic Fender tone. Today's models can be very good, and the large number of instruments available means you can try quite a few to find a bass that feels and sounds good to you.

Some other basses that have proven to be successful recording instruments:

- James Tyler fretted and fretless 4- and 5-strings
- Music Man fretted and fretless 4- and 5-strings
- Sadowsky fretted and fretless 4- and 5-strings
- Pedulla fretted and fretless 4- and 5-strings
- Warwick fretted and fretless 4- and 5-strings
- Wal 4- and 5-strings
- Yamaha TRB 5-string
- John Carruthers fretted and fretless 4- and 5-strings and SUB-1 electric upright bass
- Washburn AB40 and AB45 acoustic bass guitars
- Hofner 4-string

Dealing with dead spots. Sometimes notes on certain parts of the neck decay much quicker than others. This can be a problem when playing ballads or other arrangements that call for sustained notes. Ideally a neck should have no dead spots, but some instruments sound so good otherwise that players work around the problem. (Fenders are notorious for having dead spots between the 5th and 7th frets on the *G* string.) If your main bass has lower-range notes in primary keys (*G, C, D,* etc.) that die too quickly, consider trying a different neck. Some players replace their Fender necks with graphite composite necks by Modulus or Moses. This makes sustain more consistent, but graphite produces a slightly different tone. Don't toss out a neck until you have asked your technician about the problem.

STRINGS

Roundwound strings, developed by Rotosound's James How, are the most widely used for studio work. Rotosound's Swing Bass .45-.105 set is a good all-around choice. LaBella roundwounds are also popular, as are strings by DR, GHS, R. Cocco, and D'Addario.

With their thuddy sound and quick decay, flatwounds are reserved for specialized uses; some bassists keep a bass strung with old flatwounds for the occasional vintage tone. LaBella's James Jamerson Set is the most popular; Rotosound Jazz Bass flatwounds also work well.

Should you use brand-new strings for every session? It depends on your bass. If you're constantly being asked for more treble, you might need fresh strings. On the other hand, older strings tend to have a punchier sound, and a settled string is likely to have more stable intonation.

Your strings will last longer if you wash your hands before you play and wipe your strings down afterward with a clean cotton cloth.

It usually takes a couple of days to break in strings, and most sets last three to eight weeks and sometimes longer, depending on how you use them and on your body chemistry. Don't boil worn-out strings. Boiling may appear to liven up strings, but the resulting sound is flabby. When the notes become indistinct and you have to keep boosting the treble, it's time to change strings.

PICKUPS

If your stock pickups work well and you're pleased with the sound, don't replace them. Replacement pickups work best in basses that have insufficient output or have noise and tone problems. Sometimes new pickups can make an average-sounding bass come alive.

If your bass is noisy, it may need control-cavity shielding. To be effective in passive basses, all shielding must be connected to the ground wire that connects to the bridge. Check with your technician.

Players sometimes replace noisier stock Fender pickups with quieter EMGs. Their tone is a bit crisper than Fenders' and can be strong and cutting. EMGs require an onboard battery; the bass must be unplugged when not in use to avoid battery drain. Seymour Duncan also makes a complete line of passive and active pickups. Lindy Fralin makes vintage-style replacements, and Bartolini's extensive pickup line is popular with independent luthiers.

Remember that a great-sounding bass is the sum of its parts. If you don't have high-quality woods, hotter pickups will only make bad tones louder. Start with a bass made from better-quality alder or swamp ash for the body, a maple neck, and a fingerboard made from maple, pau ferro, ebony, or rosewood.

ONBOARD PREAMPS

Many basses feature onboard preamps with active bass and treble controls; James Demeter, Bartolini, and EMG make good onboard EQs. Use onboard EQ tastefully—you shouldn't need to add much EQ to a good-sounding bass. You might want to change your tone a little depending on the song, but listen during playback to make sure your EQ choices are working.

Change your preamp batteries every couple of months, and unplug your bass when it's not in use to avoid draining batteries. If you use a Fender bass with a built-in preamp, have a preamp bypass switch installed so you can use the bass in the passive mode, too, if the pickups allow.

CABLES

Different cable brands and types sound different, especially with passive basses. A cable's length affects tone: Longer cables add capacitance, which loads down response and reduces highs. The maximum length for your primary cable should be around 18 feet. When connecting individual units in a rack or effect system, keep cable lengths to an absolute minimum. A good cable also has proper shielding to block electrical noise, low resistance for fast response and clean deep bass, and low microphonics.

Canare's G-6 cable yields good frequency response, and Belden makes good, no-nonsense cables. The best-sounding cable I've heard is the Blackring (available from Glockenklang in Germany). It's very strong and smooth with a dense silver braid shield, cloth braid, rubber insulator, thin Teflon insulator, and small-diameter silver core that reduces capacitance. The highs are accurate and mellow with well-defined bass.

TUNERS

You need to use an electronic tuner that has fresh batteries. Korg tuners—model AT2 or better—are popular with session bassists. The AT2 has a very steady needle meter and doesn't read differently as the battery drains, a problem with some Boss tuners.

DIRECT BOXES (DIS)

Tube. If you want a round, open tone, a tube DI is the logical choice. Demeter makes a good unit; the company also offers a bass preamp/DI with an optional +4 studio output so you can go straight to tape. Manley's tube DI features a 5-position tone switch. The Tube Works DI is also popular.

Solid state. Solid state offers a clean, precise tone, and some units feature high-quality Class A designs that emulate the warmth and musicality of tube units. Countryman's all-around box shows up at a lot of sessions. Avalon's DI includes an adjustable output. The high-end Glockenklang Bass Art preamp/DI is a very good Class A unit that boasts variable output for direct-to-tape recording, a built-in EQ/effect loop section, and a unique adjustable distortion feature.

OUTBOARD PREAMPS

Along with the Glockenklang Bass Art and Demeter tube preamp/DIs, other popular units include the SWR Grand Prix tube preamp/DI, Alembic F-1X tube preamp/DI, and Aguilar DB 680 tube preamp/DI. These units feature variable outputs that allow you to go straight to tape.

In high-end studios vintage Pultec tube EQs and Neve preamp EQs are popular, as is the Telefunken V-72 tube mike preamp. The V-72 has no EQ; instead it raises an instrument's output to the proper recording level.

Preamp/DIs should be used sparingly—your bass shouldn't need much help to sound good. If you have to add a lot of EQ every time you record, your bass may need some work: Pickups, strings, and setup are likely trouble spots.

Some useful EQ points for bass are 60–150Hz, 400–750Hz, 1–3kHz, and 4–10kHz. Remember that when you boost heavily at a specific frequency, other frequencies will sound weaker. Boosting +3dB is usually enough, with +6dB or more producing a radical effect. If your bass sounds indistinct, try boosting a little between 500Hz-1kHz. If your bass sounds deep but with no low-end definition, try boosting at

120–300Hz. To put some sizzle on the top end, boost at 5–10kHz. Each bass is different, so experiment. As a rule, EQ as little as possible.

COMPRESSORS

The warm, round tone of tube compressors is preferred for bass. A favorite is the vintage Teletronix LA-2A tube unit. Older Fairchild tube compressors are revered, too—and very hard to find. The Tube Tech CL-1B is a very popular modern tube unit.

AMPS

Studio players sometimes use amps to add distortion and "air" to the bass tone. A bass sound that's too clean and hi-fi can get lost in the track, and a little distortion and midrange crunch can make your bass cut through with a more organic sound. The amp signal should go to a separate track when possible so its level can be adjusted when mixing. Close-miking usually works best because it reduces delay between the DI and amp tracks.

Vintage Ampeg B-12, B-15, and B-18 tube bass amps remain extremely popular for recording, as does the classic Ampeg SVT. The Fender "blackface" Bassman 50-watt tube head with a 2x12 or 2x15 cabinet has been used on recordings from Abbey Road to Muscle Shoals. Modern amps by companies such as Eden, SWR, and Hughes & Kettner also show up at sessions.

THE MUTE

When Leo Fender first developed the electric bass he attached a small foam mute to the underside of the bridge cover. This helped control sustain and made the bass sound more like an upright—Leo's main competition.

These days you hardly ever see a foam mute on a bass, but that sound is still viable, especially for vintage tones. Most session bassists control decay with their hands, but if you need more *thud*, use a piece of foam rubber that's 4 inches long, 1½ inches high, and 1 inch deep—you should be able to find what you need at a fabric shop. Keep the mute in your case; you might want to try it on some tracks. Place it under the strings in front of the bridge saddles.

PICKS

You might be asked to play with a pick, so practice and get comfortable with it. You need to be able to play cleanly, and your action should be high enough to avoid string buzz. A medium-gauge, quarter-sized Fender pick usually works fine.

Session great Carol Kaye suggests playing downstrokes on the downbeats and upstrokes on the upbeats. A track played with a pick can sound great, but you might need to roll off some highs to avoid getting a trebly, grinding tone. As always, let your ears be your guide.

FOUR

Setting Up Your Bass

Setup affects your bass's sound, intonation, and recordability. Proper setup starts with the frets; if they're in bad condition with deep grooves on the crowns, a setup won't cure tone and intonation problems. Take your bass to a good repair shop and have the frets leveled or replaced.

The neck should have a little bit of relief, or forward bow—the peghead should bow away from you when the bass is in playing position. Insufficient forward bow will make the strings buzz or rattle from the nut to the 5th fret. Back-bow will make all notes buzz.

To check neck relief, install new strings, tune the bass, and in a well-lighted area look at the neck from the end of the peghead down the fingerboard, particularly checking the outer strings. You may need to adjust the trussrod to correct relief problems.

Trussrod adjustment. You can set your own trussrod if you own the proper wrench—the Stewart-MacDonald catalog [800-848-2273; www.stewmac.com] is a good source for instrument tools—and if you exercise patience and caution. First, locate the trussrod nut. It will be either under the peghead plate, under the neck heel plate, or at the end of the neck at the body joint. Turning the nut clockwise tightens the trussrod, which straightens the neck. BE GENTLE. Forcing the nut will most certainly break the rod. The trussrod should be turned only a quarter of a turn each time, and the bass should be retuned after each adjustment. Some basses require taking the neck off when adjusting the trussrod. If you're not confident about doing this or any other setup step, have a technician do the work.

String action. Next, set the action, or string height, of each string by adjusting the bridge saddles. Retune after each adjustment. The *G* and *D* strings will probably be slightly lower than the *E* and *A*. Play your bass unplugged in a bathroom or other quiet small space to check for noises. You should hear no buzzes or other noise when you play hard.

Most of the bassists profiled in this book keep their action medium-high for clarity without buzzes. Don't set your action too high; find the sweet spot that allows for ease of playing and good tone with no buzzing.

Nut height. Take your bass to a technician for this adjustment unless you're experienced and have the necessary nut files. When the action at the nut is too high, the notes in the lower register may play sharp. Set the nut action so it's as low as possible without the open strings buzzing when played hard. This makes lower-register playing easier and helps the bass play more in tune along the whole neck.

If there is more than a business card's thickness between the first fret and the underside of the string, your nut action needs to be lowered. If your open strings rattle at the nut, you need to have a shim installed under it.

Intonation. Each string's nut-to-bridge length needs to be adjusted so the string will be in tune with itself. To intonate a string, play it open (or sound the 12th-fret harmonic), and tune that note using your tuner. Then fret at the 12th fret and check that note's intonation. If it's flat, turn the screw at the end of the bridge so the saddle moves toward the nut a bit, shortening the string. If the fretted note is sharp, move the bridge saddle away from the nut, which will lengthen the string. Retune the open string, and repeat the process until the open string and the fretted note read the same on your tuner.

It's a good idea to check the intonation of the first four or five fretted notes on you low strings after you set the 12th-fret intonation. If action is set properly but the low notes register sharp, you may want to reset your intonation so those notes are more in tune, since you likely do more playing at those positions on the low strings. Keeping a low nut action will make lower notes more in tune in relation to the intonation at the 12th fret.

Pickup height. The pickups should be adjusted so the string-to-string balance is even; sometimes a pickup's *E*-string side needs to be set lower. Set the height so the pickups don't hamper your playing position, and don't set the pickup closer than $1/4$" to the string, since the magnetism could decrease sustain—$1/4$" to $3/8$" clearance is usually adequate. You may need to add foam under a pickup to get the preferred height.

When in doubt about this or any other adjustment, take your bass to a qualified technician. Watch and learn so you can do your own setup. For a detailed look at setup and other instrument maintenance techniques, check Dan Erlewine's *Guitar Player Repair Guide* (Miller Freeman).

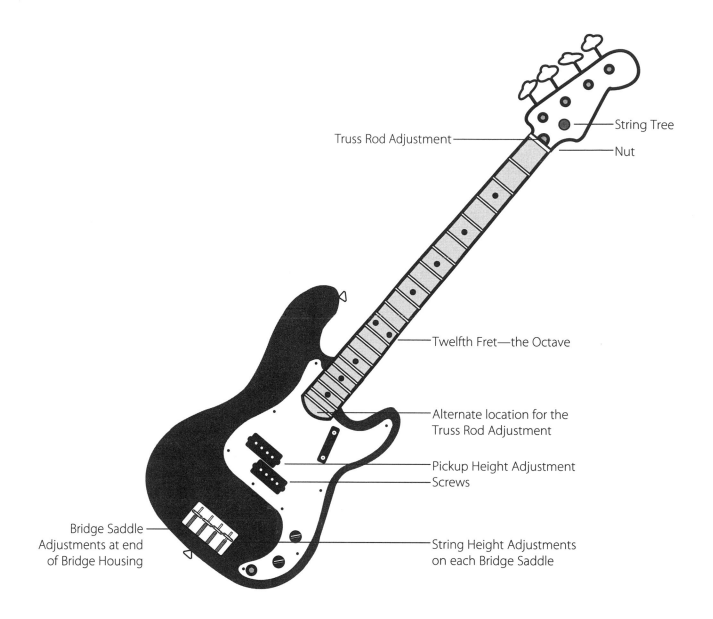

String Tree

Truss Rod Adjustment

Nut

Twelfth Fret—the Octave

Alternate location for the Truss Rod Adjustment

Pickup Height Adjustment Screws

Bridge Saddle Adjustments at end of Bridge Housing

String Height Adjustments on each Bridge Saddle

FIVE

The Number System

A must-know for any working bassist, the easy-to-learn Number System is a simple way of communicating a song. The beauty of the Number System is that it makes changing keys easy, which is essential when working with singers.

In Nashville sessions the musicians might be given a number chart of the song to be recorded, or the producer will play a demo and the musicians will have to sketch out their own charts—quickly! Since charts are transcribed as they're heard, no repeat signs are used, and most charts are written on just one page.

In the system, each note of a scale is given a number, and that number applies to the chord that's built on that note. So to use the Number System you have to know what kind of chord (major, minor, dominant, diminished) is built on each scale degree so the chord you're building your bass line from will fit in that key.

Here are the notes of the *G* major scale:

1	2	3	4	5	6	7	8
G	*A*	*B*	*C*	*D*	*E*	*F*♯	*G*

The chord built on the first note (root) of the scale is called the 1 chord; the notes are *G-B-D*, a *G* major chord. The chord built on the second note is the 2 chord, *A* minor, and so on.

Here are the types of chords built on each scale tone:

In major keys:
1 chord: major
2 chord: minor 7 (♭3, ♭7)
3 chord: minor 7 (♭3, ♭7)
4 chord: major
5 chord: dominant 7 (♮3, ♭7)
6 chord: minor 7 (♭3, ♭7)
7 chord: minor 7♭5 or diminished
   (♭3, ♭5, ♭7)

In minor keys:
1 chord: minor 7
2 chord: minor 7♭5
3 chord: major
4 chord: minor 7
5 chord: dominant 7 or minor 7
6 chord: dominant 7
7 chord: minor 7

For quick reference:

- In major keys the 1, 4, and 5 chords are major, and the other common chords are minor 7s.
- In minor keys the 3 chord and 6 chord are major, and most of the others are minor 7s.

Example A: The leader calls a tune in the key of *C* and tells the band the song has a 5-5-1-1 intro. That means you'll build your intro line on two bars of G7 (the 5 chord) and two bars of C major (the 1 chord).

Example B: The leader calls a tune in the key of *A* with "ice cream" changes (1-6-4-5) and tells you the bridge starts on a 4 chord. This means that for the verse you'll play one bar of *A* major (the 1 chord), one bar of *F♯* minor 7 (the 6 chord), one bar of *D* major (the 4 chord), and one bar of *E7* (the 5 chord). The bridge will then start on *D* (the 4 chord).

Some other rules:

- Key and time signatures are written and circled in the upper left corner of the chart.
- A superscript "7" represents a dominant 7 chord; "♪7" or "maj 7" a major 7 chord; "o" a diminished chord; "+" an augmented chord.
- In a "split bar" each chord is two beats. The chords are separated by a slash and the bar is underlined.
- A "diamond" (◊) around a number means the entire rhythm section plays a whole note on that chord.
- A circled number is a 2/4 bar.
- "MOD" means modulation; "NK," new key.
- Alternate upper structures are drawn like fractions: In the key of E, an A triad with a B in the bass would be written as 4 over a 5.
- A dot followed by a bar denotes an extra bar at the end of a phrase.
- Song form is noted by V1, V2 (verse one, verse two, etc.); CHO (chorus); and TA (turnaround).
- A sharp sign (♯) after a number shows a chromatic chord; in the key of C, 2♯ is a D♯ (or E♭) major triad.
- For bass players, the classic country quarter-note walkup from 5 to 1 is notated by four small ascending slashes.

The next page shows an example of a chart written using the Number System. Play it through in a few different keys to see how it works.

CHART USING THE NUMBER SYSTEM

Key of C

$\frac{4}{4}$

Intro: guitar and vocal only

| 5 | 4 | 1 | 1 |
| 5 | 4 | 1 | 1---- |

Band In — Verse I

1	1	4	1
5	4	1	**2/5**
1	4	1	1
4	5	1	1----

Chorus I

4	5	1	1
2	2	5	5
4	5	1	1
5	5	①◇	1----

Solo

| 4 | 4 | **4/5** | 1 |
| 6⁻ | 4 | 5 | ⑤◇ |

V – II

1	1	4	1
5	4	1	**2/5**
1	4	1	1
4	5	1	1----

C – II

4	5	1	1
2	2	5	5
4	5	1	1
5	5	1	1----
4	5	1	①

◇①   END

----	Walk up to next chord.
2 5	Two beats of 2-chord, then two beats of 5-chord.
◇⑤	Whole note on 5-chord.
①	This chord is held two beats instead of four.
6⁻	6-chord is a Minor 7th.

Other Side of the Glass:
The Producer

What do producers and engineers expect from you? What goes into making records, from song selection to the final mix? To find out we asked a couple of pros to detail the process.

PETE ANDERSON

"Bass is all about tone and time. It's not about licks."

Grammy-winner Pete Anderson has produced and played guitar on all of Dwight Yoakam's records. His production credits also include albums by Michelle Shocked, k.d. lang, and the late Roy Orbison. In the late '80s Pete changed the face of country guitar with his direct, aggressive soloing and his "blues meets Buck Owens" rhythm playing.

■ *What is the role of a record producer?*

The term is somewhat of a misnomer—if I were making films, I'd be called a director. A producer has two separate functions, much like a film director. A director works on the story—in my case the song—and he may contribute to the writing or bring in writers. He'll also work with the actors—for me, musicians—casting the film and overseeing the performances.

A producer is also much like a general contractor—the guy you hire to put in your swimming pool. The contractor tells you the cost, how long it's going to take, and hopefully what it's going to look like when it's finished. He'll also handle the paperwork and make sure everything is done properly. For me that means doing budgets to tell the record company how much it's going to cost to make the record, and working with the artist and the record company on what type of record we're trying to make and what it's going to sound like.

Of course there are a lot of other aspects. I'm a musician who became a producer, as opposed to being a former engineer. My experience was sitting with the headphones on and trying to figure out what someone wanted from me as a guitarist, so I think I have a little more empathy with what's happening on the floor with the musicians and artists.

I don't worry that much about the technical aspects of recording. I'm involved with how it ends up sounding, but I don't feel the need to have my hands on the controls. I have colors and sounds I can explain to the engineer, and he gets those for me.

■ *When you've decided a project is for you and the contracts have been signed, how do you figure out the budget?*

Most of the time the record company has a budget in mind. The budget's size depends on how big the company is and how interested it is in the artist. The budget can be anywhere from $25,000 to $300,000.

■ *How much say do you have in choosing the tunes for a record?*

It's different in every case. If you're working with a singer/songwriter, which

I've done a lot, the whole reason they got the record deal was because someone thought they were a great songwriter as well as a great singer. So you're pretty much bound by that artist's songs. At that point it becomes more of an arranging job; for instance, how do I take two good songs that sound the same and make them different?

When working with artists who are not strong writers or who are co-writers, I play a much more important part in suggesting material, co-writers, and writers to ask for material. Through the years as I've heard good songs, I've put them in the "cupboard" so I can pull them out and play them for artists who are right for them.

■ *Do you like to rehearse before you record?*

I think it's really important. I usually rehearse for five days when the budget allows. But to keep things fresh I rehearse the material only up to a point—I try to rehearse two songs a day and then move on. In one day I want to work out the tempo, key, signature licks, and major ideas I have for the song. I usually tape it so I'll remember the tempo, intro, outro, etc. I want my bass player and drummer to know what they're going to do. In rehearsals I'm not as concerned about solos and other sweetening.

■ *How many days do you typically allow for recording?*

I budget five days rehearsal, 20 days of 12-hour-days recording, and ten days of mixing, taking weekends off. I don't always use 20 days to record, though. I like the bass and drums to be done in the first four days, and then I start on the other instruments.

Lately I've been getting artists to sing their tracks earlier in the project. I used to record vocals last, but I found some artists got freaked out because they had to sing five days in a row.

During rehearsals I take notes and decide what type of bass will work best. On some songs I might want a big, fat, round, soft bass sound, on others a bright rock sound. I also might want a flatwound sound with a foam mute under the bridge, or a 6-string bass like a Danelectro or Fender VI played with a pick an octave above the main bass.

■ *Do you build a track one instrument at a time, from the drums up?*

I record the whole band at once to get a more "live" feel. I get the drum sound the way I like it, and then I go back and check each instrument as we go. During the tracking days we design each song's drum sounds by switching snare drums, kick drums, mikes, and tunings. Then we decide how the bass should play—with a pick, with round-wound or flatwound strings, on upright—and try different things to dial in the colors that help each tune sound different. If possible during tracking we'll use the bass we decided on in rehearsals. If we get a good track we can fix things while we're there and not redo the track later.

I allow the bass player the comfort of taking off the headphones and coming into the control room to do his part. Some records call for a looser sound, while others need to be very precise. So

we might sit in the control room recording bass parts for a day and a half, working on really locking with the kick drum to get that major impact of the bass hitting the center of the note with the kick drum.

Under severe circumstances when I'm cutting bass, I'll watch the kick drum's VU meter and concentrate on whether the bass is playing close to what the meter is showing me. Sometimes I'll solo the kick drum and the bass together to see how in sync they are.

The power and importance of the bass and what it brings song by song can't be underestimated. It's not so much having effects or having 5-string basses. It's a matter of knowing bass has its place and creating within the instrument's parameters. That's where the potential for expanding your career really lies. If you're the player who can come in and lay down big, fat, soft bass lines and then turn around and double them with a picked 6-string click bass, and then pick up a Jazz Bass and play it with a flatpick near the bridge, and *then* play a P-Bass with your fingers—that's what I'm looking for as a producer.

■ *What basses do you expect a player to bring in?*

If the player has only one bass, it's got to be a Fender, and I hope it would be a P-Bass. That's the definitive electric bass design.

■ *What's your technique for recording bass?*

Most of the time we record direct through a tube DI. There have been times with certain bands that we've used an Ampeg B-15 along with the DI. I leave it up to the engineer to get a good, clean sound. If you have a really good instrument that's set up properly, it will sound great.

I started using foam under the strings at the bridge early in my career and found this works well with players who don't have very good technique. You have to retune when you do this and then recheck your intonation. Sometimes I've taped a piece of foam to the nut so it hangs over a half-inch toward the pickups. This mutes the open strings and helps players who don't have enough technique to control them. I sometimes use foam even with good players because it gives the sound a good thud with no ring-over. Muting doesn't work on all kinds of music, though. Playing a ballad with foam under the strings would make the notes die off too quickly and would sound weird. For that style you want long notes. But the longer the note, the better the bass, intonation, and player need to be. Playing a long note that connects cleanly to the next is something every young player needs to work on.

■ *Do you do much doubling of the bass with other instruments?*

Sometimes on country shuffles we'll have the bass and the pianist's left hand play in unison. We also double the bass with a 6-string tic-tac bass with a pick to add a little percussiveness. Sometimes when the upright bass plays on beats 1 and 3 we'll overdub a 6-string bass playing the "and" of the downbeat.

■ *Besides talent, what makes a good session bassist?*

Part of it is personality. Successful session players have personalities that make people like them, and they make people feel comfortable and at ease—and they get the job done.

You get paid for what you don't play. If you come in and play all over the place and the producer has to keep editing you and telling you what to play, you're not going to get called again. Bass is all about tone and time. It's not about licks. It's about hitting the center of the note with the kick drum and having good tone—and being musical.

Other Side of the Glass:
The Engineer

DUSTY WAKEMAN

"I think it's just laziness when people say, 'We'll take the bass direct and it will be fine.'"

A top recording engineer and co-owner of Mad Dog Studios in Burbank, California, Dusty has engineered hits by Dwight Yoakam, k.d. lang, Roy Orbison, and Los Lobos. Along with engineering Grammy-winning records, Dusty also produces and plays bass on records by players such as Jim Lauderdale, Lucinda Williams, Rosie Flores, and Buck Owens.

■ *How has the technique for recording bass changed over the years?*

It hasn't changed on the records I make. I like a blend of new and old gear, and I love the sound of tubes. There are companies now making old-style tube stuff that's the best of both worlds. I use this type of gear a lot.

■ *Can solid state work for bass?*

Solid state can definitely work—especially for live gigs—and it can be really good for amplifiers. But for signal processing in the studio, tube equalizers and tube compressors sound more real to my ear.

■ *What bass gear do you like to see
in a session?*

A vintage Fender. I hate basses with
built-in preamps. Unless you know how
to use an equalizer, you're more likely
to mangle the sound than enhance it.
Basses with built-in preamps are also
much more likely to produce hum.
Stock Fender basses are usually ade-
quately shielded. If not, it's easy for a
good guitar tech to do the job. On my
old Jazz Bass I use alligator clips connected to a piece of wire. I clip one end
to the bridge and the other end to my
watchband between the band and my
skin. That completes the ground and
kills the buzz. With some basses, facing
a different direction can eliminate the
hum, especially if the bass has single-
coil pickups like Jazz Basses do.

If the player brings an amp, I like to
see a Fender Bassman or Showman or
an Ampeg B-15. It depends on the
music. For rock sessions I like to use
Marshall, Hiwatt, or Matchless guitar
amps for bass to get a smooth distortion
I can mix with the DI signal. Sometimes
I'll use a Fender Dual Professional
through a 4x12 cabinet instead of a traditional bass cabinet. The blackface
Bassmans also sound great—they have
the right EQ curve built in. I've got a
tweed Fender Showman head that's the
same way if you match it with the right
cabinet. I've also got a 2x12 sealed-back
Bassman cabinet I like a lot.

■ *Do you like basses to have new strings?*

It depends on the music. For rock I
like them to be brand new. For more
traditional styles, roundwounds tend to
be a little hollow-sounding until they're
broken in. Fortunately they sound new
for only about a day. For a country or
roots sound you don't need to change
strings very often. For rock sessions I
put new strings on my Jazz Bass. If I
want it bright but not as bright as roundwounds, I'll put on half-rounds or
ground-wounds. I also have a 3-string
bass with heavy-gauge LaBella flatwounds I'll probably never change. For
any track that needs a big thick bottom,
that bass is amazing. Rick Turner built
it and put in a Seymour Duncan Vintage P-Bass pickup. It started out as a
joke and now it's my main bass.

The angle of your picking fingers
against the strings can change how
bright or dull a bass sounds. A lot of
younger players don't let the string
sing—they mute it unintentionally. It's
like a drummer who can't get the stick
off the head fast enough. Getting the
plucking finger off the string quickly
allows it to sing better.

■ *Do you like a strong attack from
the bass?*

Yes. You can add all the top end you
like, but if the bassist played lightly the
track will never be punchy. On the
records I do, the bass needs to have a
sound similar to the kick drum so the
two will marry well. The basic rule of
recording is: Fix it at the source. If
you've got a great musician playing a
great-sounding bass, getting it on tape
is easy.

■ *What do you think about active pickups?*

Batteries can be a problem. Over a
couple of days the bass sound can start
changing, and when you put in a new

battery the bass becomes louder and brighter.

■ *What about rack systems?*

I don't use them, and I don't think they're necessary. Fender got it right 40 years ago—I've never heard anything that sounds better. I think racks are just toys.

■ *How do you record bass?*

I generally use a Demeter tube DI with the signal split to the board and to a miked amplifier. Or I'll use a Demeter tube bass preamp instead of an amp—that sounds really good. It's a broad-band EQ—you don't get yourself in trouble like you can with narrow specific-band EQs.

I mix both tracks down to one or, more ideally, leave them on separate tracks and not blend them till I mix. That gives me total control. For country records I go for a full, clean amp sound. For rock records I usually crank the amp way up to get some nice tube distortion. When you solo that kind of bass track it might appear too distorted, but in the track it provides a nice presence. A lot of classic rock records have a lot of distortion on the bass, and it sounds great. It makes the sound exciting.

I avoid board EQ because you can never take it off. If you have to use board EQ, there is something wrong with the source. If I need to EQ, I'll do it with the Demeter preamp. If I'm going to use EQ going to tape, I'll use a Pultec tube EQ or something similar with a broad range. The Pultec is basically a bass knob and a treble knob

like a Bassman amp, unlike board EQ, which is very specific.

I think it's just laziness when people say, "We'll take the bass direct and it will be fine." They don't spend that little extra time to turn an okay bass sound into a great bass sound. A direct can sound fine by itself, but in the track there's something missing. You need some color and distortion to give it presence and compete with the drums.

■ *What produces phase problems between the amp and DI?*

It's the polarity of the signals. A signal is either positive or negative at any given moment in a waveform, and you have to make sure both sources are in phase with each other. Otherwise you lose your bottom end. Any time you have more than one signal path for one source you should reverse the phase of one of the tracks and compare it. It will either get a lot better or a lot worse. The same goes when you have more than one mike on an instrument. You should flip the phase to see if the sound improves.

To get the DI and amp perfectly in phase, you have to take into account that the direct signal is getting to the board faster than the amp signal, which has to go through the speaker and through the air, and then to the mike. Some engineers put a little delay on the DI signal to get it totally in phase and time-aligned with the amp signal. That's taking it to the extreme, but you should always check the phase.

■ *What kind of mike do you prefer for, say, an Ampeg B-15, and where do you place it?*

I like to use a big diaphragm dynamic mike like an AKG D-12 or an Electro-Voice RE20 for a clean sound. I like to place it very close to the speaker to get a bigger sound—usually a couple of inches from the grille, slightly off the speaker's center. For rock sessions I sometimes use a Shure SM57 because it has a built-in presence that works well.

To add a little ambience you can set the mike two or three feet away. This approach sounds good by itself, but when mixed in you can end up fighting it—you have to be careful how much ambience you use.

■ *Do you mind a little string buzz?*

The string buzz you hear because you're right next to the bass usually doesn't come through. But buzzing or rattling notes can be a drag.

■ *How do you deal with low-end clashes between bass and acoustic guitar?*

A good-sounding acoustic with the mike in the right spot will not have that problem. The best spot to mike an acoustic is where the neck meets the body, about a foot away. There's a good balance there and it's not boomy.

■ *How do you keep the bass from getting lost when it's doubling the pianist's left hand or a when 6-string bass is playing along?*

The players have to work it out exactly, note for note. Piano has a bright sound, so you need a softer electric bass tone. You wouldn't want to use a pick.

■ *How do you record upright bass?*

I like to record it in a booth to contain the sound a little bit, and use a Neumann U47 about a foot away from the front of the bass. That's where the sound is more focused. If there's a pickup I take it direct and mix it in about 30 percent for presence. They're making pretty good upright pickups these days, and a tube compressor can really make the sound come alive. But much of the sound is the player and the quality of the tone coming from the bass.

■ *How do you set up a bass track for mixing?*

First I get the drum tracks sounding right. Then I add bass and try to get it to marry with the kick drum. I use a lot of compression going to tape and when mixing. For some rock records I use two compressors in series on the bass. I might set the first compressor to a slower attack time, like a 4:1 ratio, to let more of the natural attack come through before the compression starts. Then I might set the second unit at a really high ratio like 20:1 so it catches any peaks the first unit missed. This makes the bass appear to be loud in the mix; the bass never disappears, and every note is in your face.

■ *How do you make sure the bass will be heard on small radios and portable stereos?*

I mix at low levels on small speakers. When mixing on big speakers everything sounds great, but unfortunately everyone doesn't have that kind of system. EQ-wise, I try to put the main energy of the kick drum at 50–60Hz and the bass an octave above that. That way they each have their own space. I sometimes roll low-end off the bass guitar below 50Hz so there's space for the kick drum.

A lot of times after the mix is set up I add a little midrange to the bass. I try to find that sweet frequency that makes the bass pop out. The frequency I choose sometimes depends on the song's key. Sometimes it ends up around 2k. I boost the mid EQ 3dB and then sweep through and find the frequency I like. You have to trust your ears and do it without even looking. It may be something that makes no sense logically but works in the mix.

■ *What's the most common problem you run into when recording bass players?*

Timing—being able to hit the note right with the kick drum is everything. When I play I try to figure out who's playing ahead of the beat or behind it and then control my playing to match.

A lot of younger bass players don't have that concept yet. The first time you solo the bass and drums for them and they're not together, they're totally shocked because they've never thought in those terms. It doesn't matter how great your sound is—if your feel isn't there it's going to sound terrible. Not only should the parts be correct, but the performance should be almost magical when soloed with the drums. That's what makes a great bass player and rhythm section.

■ *Any advice for aspiring session bassists?*

Spend your time and your money working on your technique and becoming a great player. Don't think buying the biggest and best bass or rack is the answer. It's all about technique, your ears, and learning to listen to everyone you're playing with and hearing yourself as part of a total sound. And remember—the drummer is your best friend!

Upright Bass

A renewed interest in traditional sounds has encouraged record producers to call for upright bass more often, and many bassists are finding they can expand their session work by playing upright as well as electric. The upright presents its own challenges for playability and good tone; here are the basics in choosing, setting up, and recording an upright.

CARVED OR PLYWOOD?

Both carved and plywood basses can be good recording instruments. It all depends on the bass, strings, setup, player, and style of music.

Carved (solid wood) basses are preferred by orchestra and jazz players because of their craftsmanship and sound. The complex tone created by some carved basses is usually not attainable from plywood instruments.

Plywood (laminated) basses are popular with many rockabilly and bluegrass players because of their affordability and usable tone. Some plywood basses sound quite good, with strong volume and projection.

SETUP

Before you set up an upright, make sure the instrument is in good shape. This includes repairing cracks and holes and making sure the fingerboard is properly planed to a smooth, even finish. Unless you're experienced at such work, have it done by a reputable string-repair technician. If your area has a symphony orchestra, call their office for instrument-repair recommendations.

THE BRIDGE

I recommend installing bridge adjustment wheels, which allow you to raise or lower the action to compensate for seasonal string-height changes. Otherwise you need a summer bridge and a winter bridge. Make sure the bridge is not bent or cracked and that the feet make good contact, with no gaps between the bridge bottom and the bass top. The bridge's arch should match the fingerboard's.

The bridge's grooves should allow only the string's bottom half to sit in the groove, with the other half exposed. This provides better projection and sustain. To keep the strings from binding, squirt powdered graphite into the grooves.

The bridge should be at a 90-degree angle in relation to the top and should not lean forward or backward. Check the angle and position after putting on new strings and after transporting the bass.

THE NUT

Nut height is crucial to intonation and ease of playing. As with the bridge, the nut's grooves should allow half of the string to be exposed. Use graphite here as well. The string's distance from the fingerboard at the nut should be about the thickness of a business card. This makes playing easier; do not overlook this critical adjustment.

THE SOUNDPOST

This small wooden cylinder is located inside the bass just behind the *G*-string side of the bridge foot, wedged between the top and the back. The exact location helps determine the tone. The strings' pressure on the bridge gets transferred to the post, which then transfers vibrations from the bass's top to the back.

Your repair person will have a special tool for reaching through an *f*-hole and adjusting the soundpost. Work together on finding the soundpost-placement sweet spot that creates an even, rich tone with good string-to-string balance. The post should not be wedged in too tightly.

The soundpost must be in position at all times when there is string tension on your bass. If your soundpost falls over (because, for instance, the bridge is knocked over or the strings are all loosened at the same time), do not tighten the strings to full tension until the soundpost is repositioned. Playing the bass without the soundpost in place will most certainly crack the top. When changing strings replace one at a time, leaving the others tuned up. This maintains the tension needed to keep the soundpost in place.

STRINGS

If possible, set up the bass with old strings of the same type and size you're planning to use. This keeps new strings from being loosened and tightened many times during setup. Final soundpost adjustment should be done with the strings you plan to use.

Metal strings. Metal strings are best for attaining the bright, ringing growl jazz players favor. The most commonly used gauges are orchestra and the lighter-tension weich. LaBella makes a good light-tension rope-core string (Professional Set #7720 light gauge), and D'Addario Helicore and Pirastro Flat-chromesteel strings are also found on pros' basses. Thomastik Spirocores are also popular.

Gut strings. Gut strings produce a softer, more mellow tone and are more sensitive to temperature changes. They generally have less tension than metal. LaBella makes a popular gut string set. Most widely used is their Professional Set #980, featuring metal-wound gut *E* and *A* strings with all-gut *D* and *G* strings.

Some players like to mix and match string types and gauges. Glenn Worf puts all-metal Spirocores on one bass and mixes Spirocore *E* and *A* with gut *D* and *G* strings on another. Jazz bassist Bob Magnusson mixes Spirocore orchestra gauge *E* and *A* strings with weich-gauge *D* and *G* strings. Ron Carter uses the tape-wound LaBella Professional Set #7710 rope-core metal strings.

Start with lighter-tension strings and set your bridge height so you can play easily with no string buzzes. If you get buzzes, raise your action a little. You don't have to have high action to get a good sound.

MIKING AND RECORDING

Tube mikes and compression work well for upright when properly adjusted. Try a few mikes if possible and listen for the mike that requires the least amount of EQ. Here are a few tips on mike placement:

- Try placing the mike at the same height in relation to the floor as the bridge, with the mike directly facing the bridge about six to twelve inches away. This creates minimal delay in relation to attack.
- Place the mike a couple of feet away. This creates more ambience and allows the sound to develop. Arco or bowed bass is best recorded with the mike two to six feet away.
- If the *E* string is not as loud as the others, place the mike nearer the *E* side of the bridge.
- Blend in your pickup by recording it on a separate track. The pickup can add a nice direct tone that increases definition. Play with a firm, consistent attack. The tone comes from your fingers.

EIGHT

The Players

- Mike Brignardello
- Mike Chapman
- Nathan East
- Hutch Hutchinson
- Bob Moore
- Larry Paxton
- Dave Pomeroy
- Leland Sklar
- Neil Stubenhaus
- Glenn Worf
- Bob Wray

Mike Brignardello

*"Dynamics and groove have always been important in my playing.
That's what music is all about—the little nuances keep the ear interested."*

Selected Discography

With Travis Tritt: *Country Club*, *T-R-O-U-B-L-E*,
It's All About to Change, *Ten Feet Tall and Bullet-
proof*, Warner Bros. With Tim McGraw: *Not a
Moment Too Soon*, *All I Want*, Curb. With Giant:
Time to Burn, Epic; *Last of the Runaways*, A&M.
With Amy Grant: *Lead Me On*, A&M;
Unguarded, Reunion. With Clay Walker:
Hypnotize the Moon, Giant. With John Ander-
son: *Paradise*, BNA. With David Lee Murphy:
Out with a Bang, MCA.

Biography

Raised in Memphis, Tennessee, Mike
Brignardello is one of the modern breed of
bassists dominating the session scene. His
rock and R&B background, touring and
recording work with the rock band Giant,
and ability to play traditional country have
made him a popular studio hand with such

multi-platinum artists as Travis Tritt, Mark
Knopfler, Tim McGraw, Pam Tillis, Billy Ray
Cyrus, and John Anderson.

■ *What drew you to the bass?*

I grew up in Memphis, where bass is
such a huge part of the music. As a kid
the bass always caught my ear when I
listened to Motown and to Stax artists

like Otis Redding, Sam & Dave, and
Booker T. & the MGs. I'm not one those
guys who started out on guitar and
switched to bass because no one wanted
to play it. I started out on the bass. My

first instrument was a 3-string bass that cost $40. I made it a 3-string because someone had dropped it and sheared off the *G*-string tuning peg. Six months later I got a Vox Cougar—an old, not very good hollowbody bass.

■ *Did you have a mentor at that time?*

I was pretty much self-taught; I learned by taking lines off records by ear. I got into bands and learned the ten or twenty songs we wanted to play, and then went out and played a gig. I always seemed to be the youngest member of the bands I was in, and the older guys helped me along and showed me stuff.

■ *Did you play exercises when you started out?*

I remember a song by Spencer Davis called "Blues in F." It was a standard jazz-style I-VI-II-V thing, and I played it for days! It had a really cool bass part that walked through all the chords. If you grew up in Memphis, you had to learn the Stax songbook, which included Duck Dunn's bass parts. I also learned a lot of Motown stuff.

I learned whatever seemed hard for me to play at the time. I never really practiced scales, and I didn't learn to read bass clef until I started doing sessions. There was a sense in Memphis that no matter how good your chops were, if you couldn't groove with the drummer you weren't any good.

■ *In laying down a groove do you play on the back side or right on the beat?*

I think I put it a little behind the beat, because of my background. In Nashville

they call it the "Memphis" side of the beat. Whenever I do sessions I try to listen to the drummer to find out where he's putting it. I'm fortunate that I get to work with great drummers with very consistent time. Some drummers feel it right in the center, and some feel it a little behind or in front, and I try to immediately adjust. When the bass and drums are putting it in different places the track feels unsettled.

Doing sessions with a lot of different drummers tweaks your time radar. I'll know after working with a drummer a few times where he feels the beat, and that helps me make the adjustment. Luckily most of the drummers I work with are consistent and keep the same pocket all day.

■ *How can bassists develop time and listening skills when they have no drummer to play with?*

Playing along with records is good. Even though that world-class drummer is not there in person, he's right there on the CD. Drum machines can be a great tool to show you timing problems and when you tend to play on the front or the back of the beat. Today's machines aren't as stiff as the old ones, though a drum machine is not going to groove like a real drummer. It's also good to groove with the loops that some machines have programmed into them. I like this better than using a metronome.

■ *How did you learn to be comfortable playing with click tracks?*

I've become more comfortable as the drummers have become more comfortable. In the early '80s we started using clicks a lot, and some drummers had a hard time adjusting to them. So that affected the whole rhythm section. Players today know they have to play with perfect time and that they will be playing to clicks. There's no shortcut—you just have to do it over and over. The good drummers I work with know not to hit every beat with the click—they push and pull a little bit so the track feels more human. Studios have a cue system for headphones that allows separate levels for the instruments and the click. I usually turn the click off because I want to be sure I'm playing with the drummer and the band.

It's hard to groove a shuffle to a click. We have a joke in the studio that "the shuffle is just an opinion"—everybody puts it in a slightly different place. That's what's cool about a shuffle: It's organic, not a precise formula.

■ *What else do you practice?*

My time is limited because I work a lot, so I practice what I'm weakest on. I have an old Kay upright, and that is by far my biggest weakness—I spend most of my practice time on it. I've been playing it for a year and I'm still very much a student. Before the upright I spent a lot of time on fretless, which is another instrument I came to late. I worked really hard and now I'm more comfortable on it.

■ *How much fretless do you record?*

I use it about 10 percent of the time. It depends on the song, but if I think it's appropriate I'll use it. I work for some producers who love fretless and others who don't like it at all.

■ *Recording technology lets you hear every nuance of the bass. Does this make bassists play better with better technique?*

I think that's true for every instrument. Technique has had to keep up with technology, because you can be very exposed. I think that's helped us all become more conscious of note length, slides, and so on.

On the other hand, some of my favorite records have not been played with a technical approach. A lot of old records by the Beatles or Merle Haggard have technical flaws, but the feel is there. I try to play what moves me and the track. I'm trying to project emotion, and technique allows me to do that. But sometimes I'll leave a little sloppiness in a track if it seems to project the right feeling. A lot of players do that.

■ *So there's more to playing a part than making it accurate?*

Accuracy is the first building block, but you've got to get into the many subtleties that make a part feel good. It's something I work on daily: how I attack the note, where I release it, whether the overall note length is working. I don't know how to figure it out except by using your ears. I record myself practicing—one playback is worth a thousand words! I can immediately tell if I need to phrase a part differently, or whether I need to play a little more on top of the beat in a certain section or lay back in another. It starts with your ears; you've got to be able to hear the differences.

■ *Is reading important?*

When I first moved to Nashville in

1982 I started doing contemporary Christian records with Amy Grant and Michael W. Smith, and in that field there seems to be more reading on sessions. I realized I needed to learn how to read, so I got my act together in a hurry. I bought books and woodshedded, and also got a lot of on-the-job training. The more I read the easier it got.

For several years I did a lot of reading sessions and became pretty good at it. Then I stopped playing sessions for about five years when I joined Giant. When I came back to sessions, most of the calls were for country dates. I don't know why I started doing so much country; maybe it was because country had developed more of an edge and they were looking for someone who was a little more aggressive. Country sessions usually involve number charts, but my previous reading experience helps because I can write out the figures I'm asked to play. A lot of the charts start out simple but end up with a lot of figures written in.

■ *How do those arrangement ideas usually occur?*

They're spontaneous, which is what I love about Nashville. I was drawn here because it's real human beings playing on the records, not some guy programming it into a computer. On a typical session everyone—including the engineer—will throw out ideas. Usually the coolest idea wins. The ideas for intros, outros, and other sections are a group effort, but the artist and producer have final say. The producers usually do the hiring, too.

■ *How long does it take to record a song's basic track?*

Anywhere from all day to three songs in an hour. Some producers want two songs per three-hour session, some want one per session. Shania Twain's producer, Mutt Lange, will sometimes spend a whole day on each song. James Stroud, who produces John Anderson and Clint Black, might book two three-hour sessions and get four songs done. A lot of these tracks are complete with the overdubs finished since we normally track with all the instruments at once. [*Nashville sessions are booked in three-hour blocks; union scale is around $300 per three hours. The musical leader gets double scale, and some backup players charge double or triple scale.*]

■ *On demo sessions do you ever let mistakes go by because it's "only a demo"?*

Sometimes on a demo session writers might expect to record five songs in three hours—or more. I've even done nine songs in three hours. So there's usually no time to work out anything. But I don't distinguish between a master or a demo. I never leave mistakes on tape. Not knowingly, at least!

■ *How do you stay consistent mentally and physically during a session?*

It's hard to sit in a chair from 10 a.m. until sometimes 2 A.M. the next morning, and the players who do better seem to have a better handle on exercise and diet. I try to get to the gym several times a week; if I can't do that I'll take my dogs hiking.

■ *When you first started doing master sessions, who did you look up to in Nashville?*

I always liked David Hungate's work, all the way back to his L.A. sessions—I used to steal his licks left and right! I learned a lot from studying him.

■ *Did anyone give you advice?*

Larrie Londin, God rest his soul. He was a brilliant drummer. I learned a lot from him—more by example than anything he said, like how he handled himself on a session and how he responded to artists and producers. He was always the first guy there and was always a pro. Some of my first sessions were with Larrie, and I was working with big-time studio legends. He could see I was really intimidated, so he took me under his wing and told me that I was doing great. He made me feel really comfortable and coached me when I needed it.

■ *What basses do you bring to a typical session?*

I carry a trunk with seven or eight basses. A '65 Fender Jazz Bass is my mainstay. I also play a James Tyler 5-string a lot, and I bring an MTD 5-string, a Dingwall Voodoo 5-string, a Sadowsky 4-string and 5-string, a Vigier 5-string with a 2TEK bridge, and a Washburn acoustic 5-string with tape-wound strings and a foam mute. I use the Washburn to simulate upright when the session's not set up for it. I also use a Roscoe fretless 5-string that's amazing.

The action on my electric basses is medium to medium-high; I pull notes pretty hard. I use American Flyer taper-core roundwound strings, .045-.105 on the 4-strings with a .128 B-string for the 5's. I don't use taper-core on my fretless. On my Kay upright I use medium-tension D'Addario Helicores; they're easy to get around on and have an even, mellow sound.

■ *If you could bring only one bass to a session, which would it be?*

My '65 Jazz. I've played it on more sessions than any other bass; it sounds good no matter what. Fender basses have been used on a lot of records over the years, maybe because they punch through a track. For me, no matter what kind of track—ballad, rockin' tune, country shuffle—nine times out of ten a Fender will work. I like having other basses too, because it's important to get other colors.

■ *What do you have in your rack?*

A Neve 1082 mike pre EQ, an API 550 EQ, and an API 312 mike pre. I usually plug my bass into one of the mike pres depending on the sound I want, and from there I plug the output into an old Teletronics LA2A tube limiter. Then I plug into an old Pultec tube EQ, and that signal usually goes straight to the tape machine. The mike pres bring the bass level up to the standard +4, and I also adjust the tone myself with the EQs. The vintage Pultec tube EQ is very popular for bass. It's a broad-band equalizer that adjusts frequency and bandwidth.

I've also got an old Yamaha mixer I use to blend in effects. The mixer has meters that tell me if the signal I'm sending is too hot. That's convenient when I switch between basses that put out different levels; I like to send a consistent level from bass to bass. Usually I don't use effects, but I do have an old MXR flanger I use sometimes on the fretless, and a DBX subharmonic synthesizer that adds ultra-low end.

I've got several racks, and on busy days I'll have two going at once. On most record sessions I'll be at one studio all day. The cartage bill is paid by the record company. It costs around $85 a session.

■ *What EQ points do you normally use on the Pultec?*

I usually set it at 60Hz on the low end and 3kHz on the top. I sometimes use the mike pres' EQ as well when I need to bring up "ugly" frequencies like 400Hz, 1.2kHz, and 1.5kHz. On their own those can sound pretty harsh, but they can help a bass be heard better in a track. I normally go in and check how my bass is sounding on the playback, and that usually tells me what I need to adjust. You need to be careful with EQ because what you hear in your phones isn't accurate. I carry my own headphones so I'll have some consistency from studio to studio.

I'm also very careful about how much limiting I use. I sometimes run through the limiter but won't set it to limit at all—I just want my signal running through the tubes. There's something magical about old-fashioned vacuum tubes and bass guitar. Tubes sometimes add a bit of harmonic distortion that's very pleasing to the ear.

■ *How important are dynamics when recording?*

Dynamics and groove have always been important in my playing. That's what music is all about—the little nuances keep the ear interested. That's why I try not to use too much limiting; I want the dynamics to come from my hands.

■ *Any advice for aspiring session players?*

Don't give up. There are so many things that can discourage you, but people who have made careers in music have been able to stay focused through all of the hardships. Frustration—not lack of talent—drives a lot of people out.

I love being in the music business because there's always something to learn—you can never say you've mastered it all.

In the style of Mike Brignardello

Track 2

Mike
Chapman

"My rule is, 'The more you work, the more you work.'"

Selected Discography

With Garth Brooks: *In Pieces*, *Ropin' the Wind*, *No Fences*, Liberty. With Blackhawk: *Blackhawk*, Arista. With Brooks & Dunn: *Brand New Man*, Arista. With George Jones: *High-Tech Redneck*, MCA. With Sammy Kershaw: *Haunted Heart*, Mercury. With Kathy Mattea: *Willow in the Wind*, Mercury. With Joe Diffie: *A Thousand Winding Roads*, *Regular Joe*, Epic. With LeAnn Rimes, *Blue*, Curb.

Biography

A former Muscle Shoals session player who found success in Nashville, Mike Chapman has played on all of Garth Brooks' records. In fact, Mike has a knack for playing on multi-platinum albums; his client list includes Kathy

Mattea, Sammy Kershaw, Martina McBride, LeAnn Rimes, George Jones, Brooks & Dunn, and Blackhawk.

■ *How did you start playing bass?*

I got very excited about the Beatles when they came on the scene, and that inspired me to learn guitar. I got a guitar for my 12th birthday, and my dad taught me some things. I played in bands around town until I was 20, and I sometimes played bass by default when

there was a guitar player better than me on a gig. Then I got offered a job playing bass in a nightclub six nights a week. I borrowed a bass and an amp, and after a few months I realized bass was my thing. It seemed I could play the things I heard in my head easier on bass than on guitar. That gig had a good drummer, and he helped me learn to listen and lock in with the drums. I've stayed with bass ever since.

My first bass was a mid-'60s Fender Precision. At the time there was a bass player in town I really respected who played a Jazz Bass; I would go to the club where he played and sit in on his bass. I loved the feel of it, so I decided to get a Jazz Bass, too. I played my P-Bass for a year, and then sold it and bought a new 1973 natural-finish Jazz Bass with a maple neck. It was my main bass for years, and I still have it.

■ *What kind of gigs did you do at first?*

Around the time I was 20 I worked for two years at a nightclub in Huntsville, Alabama, playing standards for the over-50 crowd. We also played a lot of swing tunes and some light-jazz standards. We had a sax player, so I was learning to play in $B\flat$, $E\flat$, and other unfamiliar keys. I played with a country band for a couple of years and then got a Top 40 gig.

All those gigs gave me a great education and prepared me for session work. To be a session bassist you need to be able to play a little bit of everything. Sometimes when I do demos the songwriters will bring four or five songs, each in a different style.

■ *Did you practice a lot?*

I never really practiced much at home. I would go hear other bass players and try to play like them on my gig. I bought records and checked out Ray Brown and other players, but most of what I know I learned by doing it at gigs or jam sessions.

■ *Who was the first name artist you worked with?*

When I was about 25 I got a gig with Hank Williams Jr.—it was my first road gig. I spent a few months with him and then went back to playing clubs. That's when I started pursuing studio work around Muscle Shoals.

■ *What Muscle Shoals bassists did you look up to?*

David Hood and Bob Wray. I asked them about the strings and pickups they were using, and they were both nice to me. When I started playing sessions in Muscle Shoals, Bob had already moved to Nashville, so I didn't get to know him until I moved there. I stayed in Muscle Shoals for five years. I finally moved to Nashville because I was making more money there.

At first I was doing mostly publishing demos in Nashville. A couple of Muscle Shoals songwriters got deals there and were calling me to work for them. Through those guys I met other songwriters like Dave Loggins and Don Schlitz, and they started using me on their demos.

It's great doing demos for writers because you end up meeting their co-writers, and if they like you they may use you on their demos, too. My rule is, "The more you work, the more you work." The more work you do, the more people you meet, and if you're good and a nice guy you'll get more work.

When I first met Garth Brooks he was singing on demos I was playing on, and soon he started hiring me for his demos. When he got his record deal he asked his producer, Allen Reynolds, to use me. It's important to make connections, because the people you work for on demo sessions may be producers someday. I met a sound engineer named Mark Bright who was also a song plugger for EMI. He used me on his demos and eventually started working with Blackhawk. He called me to play on their records, and they did well. Now he's an in-demand producer, and he's using me on a lot of projects.

■ *What bassists did you look up to in your early days in Nashville?*

I liked what David Hungate was doing, and, of course, Bob Wray, who was doing a lot of work. But I didn't get any pointers from anyone about sessions; I had to figure it out on my own. It's not very often bassists get to meet and talk, and I was a little shy about going up to established players and saying, "How can I get to where you're at?" Sometimes I'd ask a good drummer if there was something I could do to be better. But basically I just tried to do the best job I could, not only playing-wise but personality-wise. I also tried to be on time or early. I learned you have to have talent, a good work ethic, and a good-sounding bass—more than one if possible—that plays in tune. Your bass needs to be quiet with no ground noise, and the action shouldn't be too low. It also helps to have a good tuner, and a preamp comes in handy.

If the producer asks you to play something dumb, you can offer an alternative and maybe he'll go for it. Either way, make sure he's happy. He's paying you, and if you do what he wants he'll call you back.

■ *What was your first Nashville master session?*

It was with Russell Smith, who used to be the lead singer for the Amazing Rhythm Aces. He had a solo deal with Capitol with Garth Fundis producing. It was a great album, but unfortunately no hits came from it. I also toured with Russell.

The first No. 1 record I played on was Kathy Mattea's "Burnin' Old Memories." Shortly after that I started working with Garth Brooks and Joe Diffie. I played on three No. 1 hits with Joe, and I've played on all of Garth's albums except for one song; they wanted upright, so they called Roy Huskey Jr.

■ *What style do you try to put across?*

I try to play solid with great tone. My goal is to have a tone that's going to be heard on the radio—one that cuts through. I also try to inject a little personality but not treat the song like it's my solo. I believe it's important to be a team player and not get in anyone's way, and at the same time find a spot to put in something that sets my playing apart. When producers criticize a bass player it's because they don't like the player's tone or because he plays too busy. That's something you have to learn to guard against. But some producers want you to play more—sometimes you have to be a mind-reader.

You also have to be careful not to play too much when you're cutting with just drums and acoustic guitar, because you don't know what's going to be added later. Most of the time I ask the producer what he's going to put on the track later, and I keep that in mind as I record.

When I'm tracking with a small section, I won't avoid playing the licks I hear for the song, because they're usually things I would play with a larger section anyway. If it's a rock-trio date, I might play a little busier. But I try not to overplay, no matter what kind of session it is.

■ *Where do you like the bass to sit in the groove?*

It depends on the song. If it's sad I'll generally play on the back of the beat. If it's happy I might lean forward. If the groove is behind the beat on a song with happy, upbeat lyrics, it's hard for the music to convey the mood. But there are always exceptions.

Sometimes the drummer is playing to a click right in the center of the beat, and the guitar player or someone else is playing in front. When that happens I try to wedge myself between them, because if I played strictly with one or the other, the track won't sound good. My object is to make the song and the singer sound good, and if someone else won't change, then I'll be the martyr and fill in the space.

■ *What do you listen for in a playback?*

I make sure the kick drum and the bass are locking in. I listen for "flams"—where the bass drum and bass don't hit in sync—and dragging or rushing a downbeat or lick. And most important I listen to whether it's grooving.

■ *How hard do you play when tracking?*

I play hard and use medium-high action. I used to have low action because it was easier and I could play faster. When I started doing sessions, I didn't have a preamp; I just plugged in to a DI. One day the engineer wasn't getting enough bass volume and the tone wasn't that good, and the keyboard player—who was a seasoned pro—told me if I played harder the bass would sound better. So I raised my action and started playing harder. He was right.

■ *What bass do you use most?*

A fretted Warwick Streamer Stage II 5-string with MEC pickups. My '73 Jazz used to be my favorite, but I now use the Warwick 90 percent of the time. The rest of the time I usually play my Jazz or a Warwick Streamer Stage II fretless 5-string. I also have a Carvin 6-string, a Kramer-Ferrington acoustic bass guitar, and a Glaser fretless. I know bassists who carry a lot of instruments to sessions and use a different bass on every song. If it works for them, great, but I don't switch basses very much. Instead of changing basses I'll adjust the EQ on the bass or on my preamp, and I'll turn my limiter on or off. The Warwick seems to cut through on everything; it always sounds great no matter what studio I'm in.

■ *What strings do you use?*

I use .045-.135 Warwicks on the Warwick 5's. I have Warwick strings on my Jazz now, but I sometimes use Rotosound Swing Bass or Dean Markley Blue Steels. I use Rotosounds on the Kramer-Ferrington and the Glaser, and Carvins on the Carvin 6-string. On the basses I play a lot I change my strings every month.

When I first started recording in Nashville the engineers were sort of biased toward Fenders, and a lot of them didn't want to see a new bass. And I always knew I would sound good with the Fender, so I settled for that. Then everyone started buying different basses looking for a good 5-string. Now it usually doesn't bother engineers or producers when you come in with a different kind of bass.

■ *What's in your rack?*

I plug into a Neve preamp/EQ with the output going to a Tube Tech limiter, which is off half the time. Then I go into a stereo Mor Me headphone unit with a tuner output and an output to the tape machine or board, depending on the engineer. I like to go straight to the tape machine when possible. For effects I use an Alesis Quadraverb for chorus and flange on the fretless.

The Mor Me lets me adjust my own headphone mix. I have a Quest bass preamp, and I put a mike on the drums and plug that into the Quest and then to the Quadraverb to add some effects, and take that to one side of the Mor Me. That allows me to turn up the drums, my bass, and the house mix separately in my headphones. I can also turn off the house mix if a player or singer is distracting me. That way I can listen only to the bass and drums.

■ *What are the important EQ points for bass?*

On my Neve I like to boost the highs at 1.2kHz, the mids at 360Hz, and the lows at 60Hz. If you have a bass with good midrange punch like most Fenders, then you're going to be heard in the track. If it's a ballad, then I might

add lows and take off a little high end, or maybe take out some mids for a softer tone. If it's a rocker the mids and highs will help you cut through. I hardly ever play with a pick, but when I do—usually on an up-tempo tune—I'll roll off some highs and maybe add a little bottom.

■ *Do you find time to practice?*

These days I don't practice much. I usually practice when I'm warming up, and sometimes while someone is overdubbing or between songs. My Mor Me system allows me to mute my signal to the board but still hear myself in the phones. I work a lot, so when I have time off I try to spend it with my family.

■ *Any advice for aspiring session bassists?*

Work on your technique and get rid of the buzzes and other noises. Make sure your basses are in top condition. Be easy to get along with and don't bring in a bad attitude. Listen to the music that's being played on today's records so you'll know what's expected from you. Be willing to go the extra mile. Be dependable.

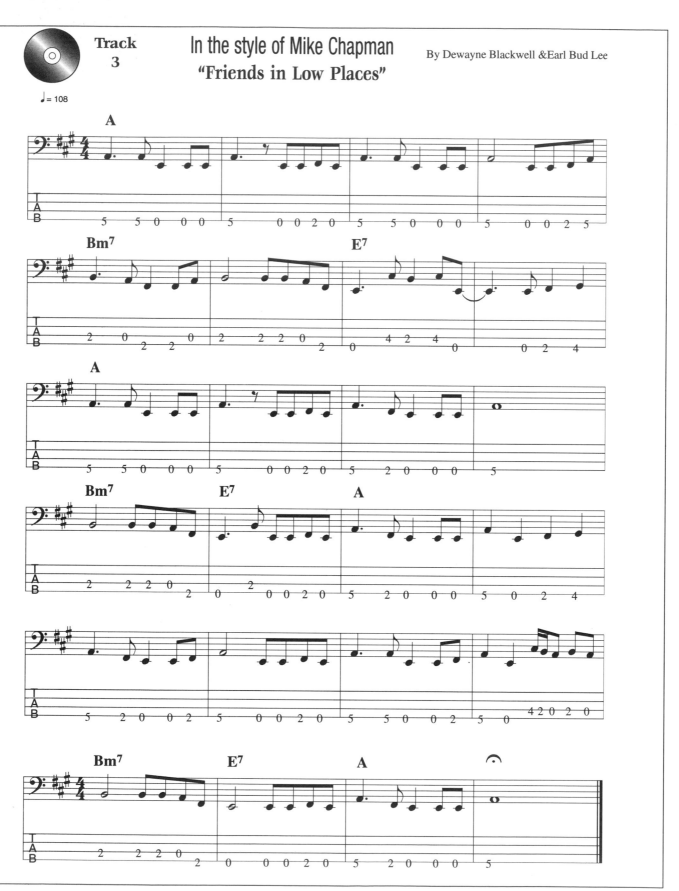

In the style of Mike Chapman
"Friends in Low Places"

By Dewayne Blackwell & Earl Bud Lee

Track 3

From the recording "Friends in Low Places," by Garth Brooks
Copyright 1990 Careers BMG Music Publishing, Inc. and
Music Ridge Music
Used by Permission

Nathan East

"I try to make sure my part is notable—that it's not only right for the song, but also represents the bass in the highest light."

Selected Discography

With Fourplay: *Elixir, Between the Sheets, Fourplay,* Warner Bros. With Eric Clapton: *Phenomenon* soundtrack, *Unplugged, 24 Nights, Journeyman, August, Behind the Sun,* Reprise. With Phil Collins: *Dance into the Light, But Seriously,* Atlantic. With Babyface: *The Day,* Sony. With Whitney Houston: *Whitney Houston, Whitney,* Arista. With Anita Baker: *Rhythm of Love, Compositions, The Songstress,* Elektra. With Kenny Loggins: *Leap of Faith, Vox Humana,* Sony. With Michael Jackson: *History, Bad,* Epic. With Quincy Jones: *Back on the Block,* Qwest. With Madonna: *Madonna,* Sire. With Natalie Cole: *Stardust,* Elektra. With Hubert Laws: *Family,* CBS.

Biography

Nathan East's strong groove and sight-reading ability have made him one of the most sought-after musicians in pop music. One of L.A.'s busiest session bassists, Nathan boasts a client list that includes Barry White, Eric Clapton, Lionel Richie, Phil Collins, Barbra Streisand, Al Jarreau, Kenny Loggins, Randy Newman, and Quincy Jones. He's also a successful songwriter and producer as well as a member of the all-star jazz quartet Fourplay.

■ *What got you interested in the bass?*

A friend put a bass into my hands at a junior high school function, and I played a lick from a James Brown song. When I looked around there were about nine or ten girls who popped up, and I thought, "This is kinda nice!" When I was in high school I used to sit outside the rehearsal-room door and listen to the bass player in the jazz band, and I was also involved in folk masses with my brothers at churches in San Diego. At one point I was tagging along and there happened to be a bass sitting on a stand. I picked it up, and it seemed at that moment I knew bass was what I wanted to do.

■ *Did you start out on electric?*

My first instrument was cello; I played it from 7th to 9th grade and used to use it as an upright! Then I started playing a little upright bass as well.

■ *What was your first electric?*

A short-scale Japanese bass called a Melody Plus. My first "real" bass was a Fender Jazz.

■ *What bassists were you into when you were starting out?*

Peter Cetera from Chicago, James Fielder from Blood, Sweat & Tears, and, of course, Paul McCartney. Some of the first records that impressed me were the albums James Jamerson and Chuck Rainey played on.

■ *Did you take lessons?*

The bassist in the high school stage band gave me pointers on fingering and other things. When he left the band I replaced him. I also got some really good inspiration watching Bob Magnusson around town. In high school I was in the jazz ensemble, chorus, and every other musical group I could join. I also played in a couple of garage bands. I

was playing everything from John Coltrane to Kool & the Gang—it was a great discovery period. I was also listening to Ron Carter, Ray Brown, Eddie Gomez, Scott LaFaro, Rocco Prestia, Verdine White, and a lot of popular groups. As far as practice I mostly played along with records and played through the Carol Kaye books. She had played on some really hip TV themes, and some of those were in her books.

■ *Did that help you when you started playing TV themes and movie soundtracks?*

I was obtaining knowledge that would stay with me for the rest of my career. I think it's important for young players to be keyed into the right music.

■ *How did you develop your jazz technique and knowledge?*

The best teacher was records. I listened to Herbie Hancock, Wayne Shorter, and people like that, just to hear what they were doing. I listened to the bass players and the soloists.

■ *How did you translate all that to your instrument?*

I was able to listen to a record a few times and pretty much get the part. You have to keep your ears open.

■ *How important has reading been in your session work?*

It was critical, especially in the early days when lot of arrangers wrote out bass parts—often very hip bass parts. Nowadays for a lot of sessions I listen to the demo and make my own chart. But it depends on the date; for TV and movie work it's imperative that you be a good reader.

- *Did you take to reading quickly?*

Yes. The best way to learn is to be in a situation where you're forced to read. In high school I memorized one of the stage-band parts and pretended to be reading, so people got the impression I was an incredible sight-reader. They started recommending me to sub for everybody, so I quickly had to get my reading together! A key to sight-reading is to try to read a bar ahead. You should also scan the chart when you first get it to find the most difficult part, so you can figure it out before you have to perform it.

- *What was your first session?*

It was for a group called the Patti Family Singers that included a young singer named Sandi Patti. I used my little Japanese bass for that record. It had a great sound—I wish I still had it. We did that album in about two days. I was nervous, but I got to go over the songs before the session. I couldn't believe I was getting paid to do something that was so exciting and that I loved to do.

My first L.A. sessions were with Barry White. They were very interesting, to say the least. He had two bass players, three guitar players, a drummer, and a keyboard player, and he would sing the parts to each player. It was a great learning experience watching him because he created some great parts. It was also great to work with top musicians. I was in awe of the scene and the players.

- *Did you ever overplay trying to impress people?*

No, I always tried to do the right thing—I actually had to be prompted to play more because I approached parts more conservatively in those days. I just tried to stay out of trouble. I was advised by some producers to play more and let them cut me back if needed.

- *What else did you learn in the studio?*

You need to have your bass in good working order. You also need to have a great attitude. And you should try to get the part right as soon as possible. I also discovered I needed to be able to use all four fingers of my fretting hand, and I needed to articulate cleanly.

- *Did you do anything to develop your sense of time?*

I practiced with a metronome and later with a drum machine. I think playing with a drum machine is one of the best things you can do, since a lot of time you have to cut tracks with a drum machine. It's also a good gauge of your time-keeping skills—you need to be aware of every note's timing.

- *Did anyone help you get your name around when you were starting out?*

Arranger Gene Page really sang my praises, and Abraham Laboriel passed a lot of work to me. Soon after that Jeff Porcaro started recommending me for a lot of things. I was in my early 20s—it was a fun and exciting time. The top bassists were Chuck Rainey, Neil Stubenhaus, Max Bennett, Eddie Watkins, Wilton Felder, and of course Abe Laboriel.

■ *Did you get any pointers
from the older players?*

I would go see Abe and Anthony
Jackson at the Baked Potato, and whenever possible I'd stick my head in at a
session to catch some guys playing.
Basically I learned by watching and listening. Abraham was a dream—I loved
everything he did—and also Louis Johnson, who was doing a lot of the Quincy
Jones records. I loved the way Louis
and John Robinson played together—I
used to turn off the lights and listen to
the interplay of the bass and drums in
my headphones when listening to their
records at home.

Steve Gadd and Nathan

■ *What was your main bass then?*

I was using a Fender Precision, and
around 1981 I started playing Yamahas.
I wanted to get a bass like Abe's. He
had shown me his Yamaha and said he
used it a lot and loved it, and that was
enough for me. My first Yamaha was a
BB3000 with a passive PJ setup. It
instantly sounded great. I used the
strings that came on it, and later started

using D'Addario XL Reds, which are
very bright-sounding. I changed strings
often because I had heard Anthony
Jackson changed his strings almost
every song.

■ *Was there a particular record
that put you on the map?*

I don't know for sure, but I played on
a record called *Family* by Hubert Laws
and had a bass solo on that, and there
was a Rodney Franklin record [*Rodney
Franklin*] I had a bass solo on—I got a
lot of calls from people saying they had
heard those. I also did *Footloose* and a
few other records for Kenny Loggins. It
was a snowball effect; I've been
fortunate enough to be working nearly
every day since 1980.

■ *In the early days did you usually go direct
and let the engineer get your sound?*

Pretty much. I left the effects to the
guitars and keyboards because they
came in with their huge racks. I figured
with all that going on the low end
needed a little purity.

■ *Do you feel it's important to change
your tone for each song, or could you
get by with a P-Bass going direct?*

A P-Bass direct is a really good starting point. But each song requires a different approach, and it's hard to know
what a song needs until you hear it.
Now I usually record with an active
bass for the flexibility and tone. These
days you also might track with synth
bass or be slapping and popping. But
you can change the sound of a P-Bass
by doing things like playing with your
nails instead of the fleshy part of your

finger, or picking closer to the bridge or the neck. It has a lot to do with touch.

■ *What basses do you take to sessions?*

I normally bring a couple of 5-strings. I record a lot with my Yamaha Motion bass, and I also use my Yamaha signature 5-string, which has two J-style pickups, a three-position switch that chooses non-active, mid cut, or mid boost, and active bass and treble controls. I also bring a Yamaha BB3000 fretless and a signature fretless, and I sometimes use a Clevinger 5-string electric upright. I've been using D'Addario Prism strings, 045-.125. I change them every other day on tour, and I like to start a session with new strings. I keep my action medium-high—enough not to buzz, but not too high so I can get around easily.

■ *How often do you use an amp in sessions?*

Maybe 40 percent of the time. Most of the time I like to go direct, but some engineers like to use a blend of amp and DI. My amp is an Eden World Tour 800 head with two 4x10 cabinets. It sounds gorgeous. I have a rack with some effects, but normally I just carry my own direct box, which was made for me by Beno May at A&M studios. It's basically a solid-state box with a huge transformer; it gives me a warm, fat sound.

■ *Do you ever ask the engineer to change your tone?*

Yes; I've asked them to add a little lows, mids, or highs depending on what I was hearing. Your sound changes from studio to studio, and sometimes you need to let the engineer know what you need.

■ *What's your right-hand style?*

I play mostly between the neck and the first pickup. I try to keep consistent while not playing too hard. If you play an active bass too hard it can distort and not blend smoothly with the other instruments. I don't often use a pick— maybe just on percussive parts or eighth-note things. I usually use my fingernail as a pick. When I'm slapping I like to hit my thumb between the neck and the first pickup.

■ *With Eric Clapton are you asked to play specific parts?*

I pretty much come up with my own ideas. Eric's sessions are really creative; normally there aren't any limitations put on what I do. Eric's a wonderful musician and a great person, and he's become a close friend. Most of the time in the studio there's a lot of laughing and a lot of great music going on. They are the most enjoyable sessions you could ever wish for.

■ *What's your mind-set when you start to track a tune?*

Usually it's to play the best part for the song, something innovative that pushes the music forward and makes it live forever. I try to make sure my part is notable—that it's not only right for the song, but also represents the bass in the highest light. I feel it's our responsibility as bassists to keep taking it to the next level.

■ *What do you listen for in a rhythm track?*

The tightness between the bass and drums and the musical content—if it's interesting and if the part suits the song and mood. Basically I'm listening for the vibe.

■ *Do you have to correct your part by punching in very often?*

I try not to. Obviously if there's a wrong note it needs to be punched in. There are many times I feel I could have played even better than what I played; in those cases I punch in just to take it up a notch. When you're listening back and not playing, you can get a really clear picture of what's happening. I punch in only to make it better.

■ *Do you ever question your ability to deal with the daily demands of studio work?*

No; I've always been excited at the challenge of new music and of my contribution and growth. My work is demanding from a time standpoint, but from a creative standpoint I feel I'm not spreading myself thin—I'm spreading myself thick with a wealth of frames of reference.

■ *What lessons have you learned in your career?*

You have to bring a great attitude to each situation. People place a lot of value on that. It's also important to listen and keep growing and to learn as much as you can while you have the opportunity. Last but not least, you need integrity and quality of the highest order.

In the style of Nathan East
"101 Eastbound"

By Nathan East & Marcel East

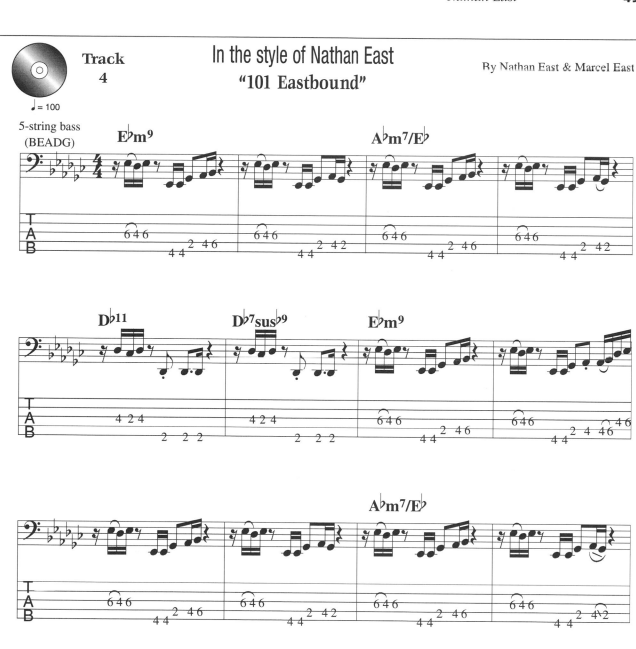

From "Fourplay" Warner Bros. Records. Used By Permission
Copyright- Neweast Music ASCAP & Eastborn Music ASCAP

Hutch Hutchinson

"If you play something you don't like and it ends up selling millions of records, hearing it all the time can drive you crazy."

Selected Discography

With Bonnie Raitt: *Luck of the Draw*, *Nick of Time*, *Longing in Their Hearts*, *Road Tested*, Capitol. With the B-52's: *Good Stuff*, Reprise. With Marc Cohn: *The Rainy Season*, Atlantic. With Roy Orbison: *King of Hearts*, Virgin. With Bob Seger: *The Fire Inside*, Capitol. With Ivan Neville *If My Ancestors Could See Me Now*, Polydor. With Willie Nelson: *Across the Borderline*, Columbia. With Boz Skaggs: *Some Change*, Virgin. With Ringo Starr: *Time Takes Time*, Private Music. With Kathy Mattea: *Love Travels*, Mercury. Various artists: *Rhythm Country & Blues*, MCA.

Biography

James "Hutch" Hutchinson calls himself a "20-year overnight success." One of the top session bassists in pop and R&B, Hutch gradually built a solid performance career that blos- somed when he was called to work for Don Was on Bonnie Raitt's multi-platinum 1989 album *Nick of Time*. His inspired bass lines have also graced sessions for artists such as Joe Cocker, Jackson Browne, the B-52's, Marc Cohn, Vince Gill, Willie Nelson, and Bob Seger.

■ *When you were playing with different bands in the '80s, did you plan to end up playing sessions?*

I knew I wanted to; I had had a goal of doing that since the early '70s.

■ *Were you studying any bassists?*

A lot of people, particularly the Memphis bass players: Tommy Cogbill, Duck Dunn, and Leroy Hodges of the Hi Rhythm Section. Cogbill was an amazing player. He and Reggie Young and other Memphis players came from a rockabilly/country background, but they were R&B players as well. I also checked out George Porter of the Meters

■ *Has being able to play different styles helped you be successful?*

I think it has, I also think it's because I know basic styles like R&B, folk, and country. Listening to and having been involved in Latin, African, Cuban, and West Indian music for many years has definitely enhanced everything else. I forced myself to listen to music I wasn't receptive to initially, and I think that's broadened my horizons.

■ *What did you practice when you first started playing bass?*

I mostly learned parts off of R&B records and then played them with bands. I was playing in groups when I was 11, six months after I picked up an instrument. I saw Wilson Pickett's band at that time, and it totally blew my mind.

■ *How important has practicing been throughout your career?*

From the time I was 12 to around 30 I practiced a lot. I work a lot now, so I'm always playing. When I get a day off I like to hike, read, listen to music, or investigate new forms of music. If I'm out of town I go to museums and art galleries. Sometimes I search for new instruments. It's important to have a life apart from music.

■ *How are your reading skills?*

I played the cello when I was younger, and I learned to read then.

Now about 30 percent of the charts I get are notated. The rest are just road maps with bits of notation. Jingles require reading, but I don't do many of those; I mostly do records and singles for soundtracks. TV and film dates are usually notated. I did some work on the movie *Toy Story* that was notated, but most producers tell me to forget the chart unless there is a key passage that needs to be played with the orchestra.

■ *Was there a single connection that put you on the map as a session player?*

I think it was because of the years I spent with the Neville Brothers and the time I spent working from Memphis to Austin and in New Orleans. It's been a gradual process. People in the industry become more and more aware of you over a long period of time. The one project that put me over the top was *Nick of Time*. It swept the Grammys that year. Don Was and I developed a rapport because we have similar beliefs about music.

Even after *Nick of Time* it took a long time to start getting calls from other producers. Don was able to give me only so much work; you need a stable of producers to make the business lucrative. A year and a half later I was still crying on the shoulders of Michael Rhodes and Bob Glaub, wondering when I was going to get more work. They would tell me not to worry, the work would come.

Patience is your biggest virtue. It will come if you do the work and have the right attitude, and if people get along with you and drummers like to work with you. Fortunately, drummers like playing with me.

■ *With all of the great players on the scene, is it easy to get lost in the shuffle?*

Personality is what makes a player interesting. Anybody can play the right notes; the nuances are what you appreciate. I'm definitely an individual, and I have developed habits over the years that have become part of my musical personality. For example, I slide around a lot. Those kind of things become your style.

■ *When you approach a track do you try not to play your same riffs?*

I do, but it still comes out sounding like me. The other day I was playing on a record with Jim Keltner on drums, and he told me everything I do sounds like New Orleans. On another session with Keltner I was doing a lot of slides, and he said Lee Sklar and I were the only guys with the courage to do that all the time. I thought that was a great compliment.

■ *What do you do if you hate a track but the producer loves it?*

If the producer likes it you generally don't have a chance of changing it. On Bonnie's song "A Thing Called Love," I never would have played that line if I had known how sparse that track was going to be. I've questioned things on tracks for Don Was, and he thought I was insane because he liked it. If you play something you don't like and it ends up selling millions of records, hearing it all the time can drive you crazy. Or sometimes you'll listen to it

six months later and it sounds okay after all.

■ *Are you easy to work with?*

I think so. If people don't like you, they're not going to hire you. Nashville producers have told me they hire people they like to be with. I have friends in Nashville who hire me because they like to see me now and then, and because I might do something a little different from some of the players there. But along with personality, you need to know the recording process; engineers like to work with a bassist who gets a good tone. You also need to know how to punch in to fix a track. I love to do that; I have a joke going with a couple engineers that I like to leave a couple of mistakes so I can fix them later!

As a young player I learned about the recording process working at Mickey Hart's studio in San Francisco. I later played on quite a few publishing demos; that's good experience because of the freedom involved. But any kind of recording experience helps. I've played on a lot of demos with drum machines, and that helped me learn to play in the front or the back of the beat—whatever a track needs. Playing with great drummers like Zig Modeliste and James Black has helped me, too. Jeff Porcaro and Jim Keltner were like mentors to me. Jeff was very encouraging; I've never played with a drummer who made a bass player's life so easy. He had perfect time and feel, and we just locked.

■ *What basses do you take to a session?*

My old P-Bass, a Modulus, a Washburn AB40 fretless, a Sadowsky fretless

5-string, a Modulus 5-string, a Kay or a Hofner, and a Music Man 5-string.

■ *How do you decide which bass to use?*

I go with what I feel, and I ask the producer what he thinks. A lot of the producers who use me are bass players; being hired by Don Was and Emory Gordy Jr. is very flattering, and it's great having their input.

■ *If you had to choose only one bass to bring to every session, which would it be?*

For the moment my favorite is my '56 "transition" P-Bass, although my Stars Guitars PJ with a graphite neck and EMG pickups always seems to come through. I use EMGs in basses I've had made and in my Modulus basses. I like those pickups because they have that Fender sound; an engineer at Capitol thought my old Stars Guitars PJ was an actual P-Bass. I leave the stock pickups in my Fenders

■ *Why do you use graphite necks?*

They don't warp, there are never any dead spots, and they are very even-sounding. I've fooled a lot of people into thinking I was using wood-neck P-Basses. But I'm still a Fender guy. I also have a few low-end basses like Kays and Harmonys that I like to throw in from time to time.

■ *What string height do you prefer?*

It depends on the bass; I own more than 50 basses at this point. I've got some old P-Basses with flatwounds and high action, and I've got some Modulus

Graphites with roundwounds and low action. Different basses and action make me play differently; I use what works best on each instrument.

■ *Do you like new or old strings when recording?*

It depends. On a Joe Cocker record I just played on, I used a '56 P-Bass with very old roundwounds, and on another track I used a new Modulus 5-string. I confused myself because it sounded like the same bass on both tracks.

■ *Do you EQ your bass when recording?*

Yes. I've been playing through an Aguilar tube bass preamp and a tube limiter. That allows me decide what sound goes to tape when I play different instruments. I bring my own head-phones, too—I think that's important. I also bring an SWR Redhead amp that gets miked.

■ *How do you EQ when you play with a pick?*

I add low end and roll off some highs.

■ *Do you do much rehearsal for record dates?*

I don't usually rehearse for records. I don't think rehearsing is healthy, because a lot of the recording process should be spontaneous. The best records I've played on have been done in a few days. If you've assembled the right players you're halfway there—very rarely will there be more than three or four takes of a song. Usually the first take is the best.

■ *Do you like to stand when tracking?*

I like to move around a lot when I play. I'll sit for certain things, but usually I end up off the chair.

■ *What do you listen for in a playback?*

I mostly listen to the overall sound. I also listen to how I'm fitting in with everything else and to the groove. Grooving with the drummer is very important. Some people can get into their own world and not be sympathetic to what needs to be done to make it a complete track.

Bill Wyman and Hutch

■ *How important is note length?*

Very important, especially in country music and when playing something basic. I'm into each note having a definite beginning and ending. I don't think about it so much now, but it was something I used to work on a lot, especially

years ago in Austin when I was working with blues, R&B, and country bands. Sometimes I'll connect every note; that's why I slide around a lot—to keep a continuous flow.

■ *How does the future look for session bassists?*

Years ago there was less work than there is now. People think there was more, but I think there were fewer players. I think it's healthier now than it's been in a long time. There are just so many players that people get disappointed sometimes. Networking is important. You can say to yourself, "I'm just going to be a player," but it is a business. It's how you get work and expand your horizons and business contacts.

■ *Any advice for the next generation of session bassists?*

In my late 20s I was questioning whether I was doing the right thing. I just realized it was what I really wanted to do, and that I wanted to keep pursuing it. Everybody in this business has some hard times, whether they come early, late, or in the middle. When I was 18 I was in a band with a major record deal, and then later there were lean years, but I've always had a good time. I've always been lucky enough to play with good people, and I never had to take a day job. If you really feel like you have the talent, go for it.

In the style of Hutch Hutchinson
"Tangled and Dark"

Track 5

By Bonnie Raitt

♩ = 98

Repeat To Fade

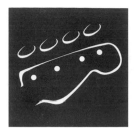

Bob Moore

*"The bass should be the bottom of the band.
It's not meant to be a solo instrument."*

Selected Discography

With Patsy Cline: *The Patsy Cline Story*, MCA.
With Willie Nelson: *The Early Years*, Liberty.
With Loretta Lynn: *Honky Tonk Girl: Collection*,
MCA. With Marty Robbins: *The Essential Marty
Robbins 1951–1982*, Columbia. With Lefty
Frizzell: *American Originals*, Columbia. With
Elvis Presley: *The Number One Hits*, RCA. With
Roy Orbison: *The Legendary Roy Orbison*, Sony.

Biography

Possibly the most recorded bassist ever, Bob
Moore has played on more than 18,000 sessions. During the 1950s, '60s, '70s, and early
'80s, he tracked with virtually every major
artist who recorded in Nashville; it was not
uncommon for Bob to play on 26 sessions in
one week. In addition to his country work
Bob was also in demand as a pop and rock &

roll bassist for such artists as Elvis Presley and
Jerry Lee Lewis.

■ *How did you get started playing
the bass?*

When I was about ten years old I
wanted to be a singer and a guitar
player. My two best friends got a guitar

and a steel guitar for Christmas, and the
three of us wanted to start a band, but
we didn't have a string bass. I found
one, so I became the bass player. I
believe that was around 1944 or '45.

The first upright bass I actually owned was a Kay Swing-Master with gut strings.

We called ourselves the Eagle Rangers, and we became well known around Middle Tennessee for our Sons of the Pioneers harmonies and for performing popular tunes.

During summer vacation I would go out as the bass player with tent shows. Sometimes during the show I would sing a song while playing guitar, and then go back to the bass. It was just like a circus. After doing those kinds of jobs I started getting a reputation for being a good bass player, and I started getting calls to do more things. I started playing with guitar players like Jabo Arrington, Hank Garland, and Grady Martin. Jabo was one of the best guitarists around. Hank and Grady copied his simple, hard-driving style. Jabo also helped me get work in the music field, as did Grady Martin.

At 16, having already done some touring and radio shows, I moved into a boardinghouse and shared a room with Hank Garland. Hank was one of the finest guitarists ever in country music— and one of the top jazz players as well— before an auto accident left him partially brain-damaged.

Hank got me into playing jazz, and we formed a group and started doing radio shows. One thing led to another, and I went on the road with Little Jimmy Dickens. I learned to know exactly where "one" was at all times— because he would sometimes come in on two-and-a-half! So I learned when to adjust and when to stand my ground. I controlled the beat when I played

because that's my personality, which was formed by working with people who didn't know about meter. You might say I'm a perfectionist. I won't do anything unless I can do it well.

I stayed with Dickens for a couple of years and played on his records, which incidentally was some of the first recording work I had done.

■ *Did you have a teacher when you started?*

No, but in junior high I started playing baritone horn in the marching band, and I learned about reading. But I really learned how to read by being thrown into a big band. It was either swim or drown. I was about 20 years old. I already had some spot experience on a couple of radio shows and had played with some jazz groups in the clubs. So I had some knowledge of the songs I would be playing, and that along with the ear I had developed helped me do well on the big band jobs. That experience helped me learn to read pretty well.

■ *Did you know bass playing was what you wanted to do for a career?*

I knew I wanted to be in the music business from the very beginning. From the time I was 15 years old I knew the bass was for me.

■ *What bass players influenced you?*

It depends on what age you're talking about. When I was very young some of the bassists that impressed me wouldn't have later on. I was still impressed with Eddie Safranski, who played with Stan Kenton on his big "Opus" tunes, and I also liked Ray Brown, Red Mitchell, Oscar Pettiford, and Charles Mingus.

I didn't have an idol in the country field. However, there were a lot of players who each had a gimmick I might have stolen. I remember a bassist named Achey Burnes who did a particular kind of slap that nobody else could do. So I watched him and then practiced it till I could do it better than he could. Same thing with Joe Zinkan, Roy Acuff's bass player. He's probably the best slap player I've ever heard.

■ *What was your first recording session?*

It was in Cincinnati with Paul Howard and the Arkansas Cotton-Pickers, a Bob Wills-style group doing the songs "Texas Boogie" and "Horace the Cotton-Picker," a take-off on the traditional song "Hora'sta'cato." I was 16 at the time.

We played "Horace" on the Grand Ole Opry and tore the house down. We had drums on that show, and the Opry tried to throw them off the stage because drums weren't allowed. When they introduced us the drummer just picked up his drums and walked out and started playing, so there was nothing they could do about it.

I also recorded With Cowboy Copas during that period. Copas and Howard were on the King label.

■ *You left Dickens in 1951, married, and moved to Houston, Texas, where you did some radio shows. Then you moved back to Nashville. What happened next?*

I got a job in a nightclub with Hank Garland and Billy Burks—we had a hot little quintet, and Billy ended up being

my dentist later on. Eddy Arnold called me to work with him in Miami; Andy Griffith was on the show too, working as a comedian. When I got that job my name was mentioned in the local papers; it was considered very prestigious. It helped my career a lot.

After that the radio and TV work in Nashville started picking up. Club work at the Carousel with Chet Atkins and other things got my name around, too.

I moved to New Jersey for a year with my then-wife, who thought I should settle down and get a "real" job back in her hometown, delivering bread door to door in snow up to my hips. I hated it. So we came back to Nashville and I took a job at an airplane assembly plant. Even under those circumstances, I was happy just to be back around my buddies.

Six months later Red Foley called me. Red had the only network show on the Opry, but he was so upset over the death of his wife that he gave it up to go on the road. Grady Martin was working with Foley and recommended me for the job. At this point I was getting many different calls, and my money situation was picking up and I was doing pretty well.

Marty Robbins came to town with a series of "transcriptions" to do—256 to be exact. A transcription was a big record—this was before tape—16 or 18 inches across recorded direct to disc. If you made a mistake, too bad. You had to be on your toes. The disc held 15 minutes of music and we would fill it up.

I was also doing transcriptions for Red Foley on Thursdays and Fridays every week in Springfield, Missouri. Mondays and Tuesdays were reserved for Robbins. I did this for well over a year.

Sometimes we would record in Nashville with Foley, and Owen Bradley would be the leader on the session. One night we were jamming at a session when Owen looked at the drummer, who was his band manager, and asked him if he thought I could carry the band. The drummer said, "Without a doubt." Bradley then asked if I wanted to play with his big band. I said I would like to if I could get some recording work. He said he would see what he could do.

Bassist Ernie Newton was doing what little recording there was for Owen at that time, maybe one or two sessions a week. Owen started moving me in on some of Ernie's sessions, and it grew from there. Chet Atkins got a deal with RCA; I had already been doing Chet's sessions in his garage on weekends, putting out two or three albums a year. Next thing you know, I'm knee-deep in record sessions. I ended up working 12 years without a day off, sometimes doing as many as 26 record sessions a week.

■ *When you did transcriptions did you use headphones?*

No; it was exactly like doing a radio show. You would run through it once and make some notes if you needed to, and then they would say "rollin'." They recorded the rhythm guitar, drums, and bass all on one mike, and you would stand where they asked you to so they could get the volume right. I could hear myself fine. The recording process seems to have gotten away from the finesse of playing an instrument at the correct level. Whether it's electric or acoustic, if you play too hard or too soft, you lose something.

■ *When did recording change from transcriptions to tape?*

Around the time Patsy came to town; maybe 1952 or '53.

■ *What was a typical Patsy Cline session like?*

Everybody would gather at the studio, and Owen Bradley would ask Patsy what song she wanted to do first. She would usually say she wanted to do something easy to get warmed up. Owen would then sit down at the piano and show us the song, and we would work it up. We learned it on the spot with no chord charts. Within an hour we would have a song finished.

Patsy was a sweetheart, and she could cuss, too! We had a softball team, and Patsy would bring us cases of beer in her car—she was our biggest fan. We would go over to where she sat in the stands and drink beer with her, just talking and kidding around. She was one of the boys.

■ *In the sessions did you have to play with a firm attack in order to be heard in the track?*

I played firm because that's the way I play. It was not so I could hear myself. I was born with a crooked forefinger, so when I play, I play with the whole side of my finger.

■ *Ray Brown does the same thing.*

That's right. Ray and I talked about that one time.

■ *Did you alternate the first two fingers of your plucking hand for faster passages?*

Yes, and I have played with all the fingers of my right hand, including my thumb. It depended on what I needed to do.

■ *As you did more sessions did you develop a preference for certain mikes?*

It depended on where I was recording and who the engineer was. Some engineers wanted to please the musicians, and some wanted to tell you what to do. If I thought the mike wasn't sounding good, I would ask the engineer to use an RCA 44 [a ribbon-style tube mike]. It's the best recording mike that's ever been used for upright bass. It's that big square one you see in old movies and radio shows.

■ *You had five different string basses and kept four at different studios. Was that just for convenience?*

That was part of it. The other reason was so I could set up a bass to sound good in a certain studio. I had some basses that sounded great in Bradley's Barn but didn't sound good at RCA. I found them all by trial and error.

One of my basses was for big band jobs—it had zinc-wound gut E and A strings and plain gut for the D and G. On most of the studio basses I used gut, but sometimes I used metal-wound gut on the E and A. Those work well because they are a little more taut and they sing better, but I'm not sure they

have the bottom of a plain gut string. I used LaBellas.

When gut strings get nicked you can wipe them with very fine emery cloth. This takes off the nicks and makes the strings feel good. You can also put a little banana oil on them every now and then. This makes gut and metal-wound gut strings play more comfortably.

■ *How did you like your action?*

It depended on what I was playing. If I was playing bluegrass, I would loosen the strings and raise them up an inch or so by moving the bridge closer to the fingerboard. If I was doing a slap session, I would lower my strings by sliding the bridge towards the tailpiece. If your strings are too high they won't slap back down and hit the fingerboard.

■ *Elvis's bass player, Bill Black, loosened his E string for a percussive effect. Did you ever try that?*

I tried it all. A lot of bass players did that—they played on only three strings and used the loosened low E for slapping. But I've always believed in playing in the lower register because the bass should be the bottom of the band. It's not meant to be a solo instrument.

■ *Did you ever take more than one bass to a session in case you needed a spare?*

No, but I've actually tied a broken string back together and used it. Usually a string will break up above the nut at the tuner, so you can tie it and still be able to play.

■ *Were you making good money for your session work?*

I was making union scale and working all the time, so it was pretty good money. But I didn't just play sessions. I liked to do other things, too, like flying to London to play the Palladium or flying to Hollywood to play on movie soundtracks for Elvis Presley. When I went to California to do a soundtrack I charged double for studio time plus a first-class round-trip plane ticket, hotel room, and $100 a day. If I could do it all again, I would have asked for double scale for everything, but in those days it was unheard of.

■ *How did you learn to play so in tune?*

Playing with Little Jimmy Dickens helped me learn to play in all the keys. He used a capo, and you never knew where it might be sitting.

You have to force your fingers to feel where the notes are. Playing with a bow makes you even more accurate.

■ *Did you practice when you had time off?*

When I was younger I did. Sometimes when a new song came along with nice changes, I would learn it and then practice it in every key. I did that a lot.

■ *You played electric bass on many hit records. What did you think about the electric when it first came out?*

For a long time I didn't like it because it didn't sound like a bass. I couldn't hear any real bottom. The first time I played electric bass was on the Jim Reeves song "He'll Have to Go." It was a Danelectro 6-string. Then I got a Fender Jazz Bass, one of the first ones—

I still have it. I used flatwounds on it. On some sessions I would double, playing standup and Fender on different songs.

■ *Buddy Harmon was the drummer on a lot of the records you played on.*

Buddy is a fantastic musician. He was doing a lot of the same things I was doing. When I came back to Nashville from New Jersey, the club gig I took with Hank Garland included Buddy on drums. Buddy and I also played in a strip club together three or four nights a week, midnight to 3 or 4 in the morning, for a year. Some nights we would go out at 5 a.m. and go water-skiing. We would sleep two hours and work 22. We were the best of friends.

■ *You were the timekeeper of the rhythm section. How did Buddy feel about that?*

Buddy loved it, but I wasn't the time-keeper alone—we did it together. But Buddy was flexible and he listened. I tried to show drummers where "one" is every bar. Buddy had no problem with that; he wasn't headstrong like some players could be. After us working together for years, I didn't think about what he was going to play—I knew what he was going to play.

■ *What were Elvis Presley's sessions like?*

They were great. I loved working with Elvis; he was a nice guy. He always had a funny story to tell, and we were always wrestling and throwing each other around. We kidded and poked each other, and we played cards and told dirty jokes. He always had a bunch of his friends with him.

■ *Did Elvis's entourage make you uncomfortable?*

Oh, no, I was very comfortable with them. They were funny like circus clowns—they were yes-men. When Elvis took out a cigarette, 14 lighters would go up in his face. When we listened to a playback, the bridge would come along and Elvis would sing a high note and his friend Lamar Fike would whistle and say, "God a'mighty, that was wonderful!"

■ *When was your last master session?*

Around 1985 I started slowing down my schedule. During that period I also produced an album for Jerry Lee Lewis and one for Johnny Cash, which was the last record I played bass on. That was 1988 or '89.

In my later years I got kind of cranky because I was tired—mentally more than physically. It's important to be nice to people. When I was young and charging up the ranks and until I was in my 50s, I never met a person I didn't like. My attitude was, "What can I do to help you?" That's just the way I am.

■ *How did it feel to hear your bass lines on the radio or on a jukebox?*

It felt just like it does right now—it's my salvation that I was able to do that. I imagine it's tragic to be a man who is retired and never hears or knows or feels anything from what he did his entire life. It's a thrill for me to hear what I've done. I stop and think, "Hey, that's me."

Track 6

In the style of Bob Moore

Country Shuffle

♩ = 150

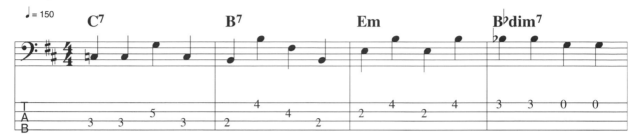

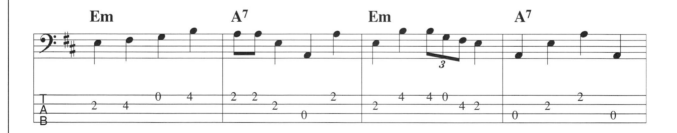

Courtesy Of Bob Moore
Used By Permission

Larry
Paxton

*"Even when playing the simplest song with just whole-notes,
make sure that they're very good whole-notes!"*

Selected Discography

With K. T. Oslin: *80's Ladies*, RCA. With Alabama: *Mountain Music*, *40 Hour Week*, *Just Us*, RCA. With 4 Runner: *4 Runner*, Polydor. With Sammy Kershaw: *Don't Go Near the Water*, Mercury. With Clay Walker: *Clay Walker*, Giant. With George Jones: *High-Tech Redneck*, MCA. With Alan Jackson: *Don't Rock the Jukebox*, Arista. With Pam Tillis: *Homeward Looking Angel*, Arista. With Joe Diffie: *Honky Tonk Attitude*, *Third Rock from the Sun*, Epic.

Biography

A session bassist who has recorded on the East and West coasts, Larry Paxton is one of Nashville's top studio players. In addition to his work on records by Alabama, George Strait, K. T. Oslin, Ricky Skaggs, Sammy Kershaw, Reba McEntire, the Nitty Gritty Dirt

Band, and Doc Watson, he also works as the staff bassist on TNN T.V. shows.

■ *How did you get started on bass?*

I started on piano and violin when I was seven or eight years old, and later on when Elvis was popular I got a guitar. My dad was a high school band

director, and as I got older I became the utility player for his different bands. He also got me to play the tuba. I played it in the stage band; it was really embarrassing to play swing and walking lines on a tuba instead of a bass! He finally got me a string bass and gave me an instructional book. I also took a couple of lessons from the bass player in my dad's band. I started playing string bass in the stage band and on weekend gigs when I was about 13. I learned to read charts during this time, too.

I started playing in organ and piano trios before I even learned to drive—I had to be picked up and taken to jobs. One night in 1961 we played in a club where we had to set up above the bar. I couldn't get my bass to fit between the stage and the ceiling, so I ran out and paid $90 for a '57 Fender P-Bass that I still use today. I hardly ever touched the string bass after that, partly because of Monk Montgomery, who pioneered playing jazz on a Fender.

■ *Who were some of your influences?*

When I first started it was Monk Montgomery, Ray Brown—any of the jazz guys. When I was in my teens everybody was into jazz.

My next big influences were Jim Fielder and Paul McCartney. Around that time I had a life-changing experience. I was in a band doing Crosby, Stills & Nash tunes and other popular songs, playing through an SVT really loud and overplaying like crazy—I filled more than the guitar player! Someone taped a performance, and we went home and drank beer and listened to the tape. What I heard myself playing was so gross that it actually changed my life. I was all over the neck playing tasteless crap, and I was so ashamed that the next day I woke up a different guy. I started playing *bass* from that

point on. So recording yourself is a good learning tool!

■ *Tell me about your early sessions.*

Between 1967 and 1971 I played a lot of rock & roll guitar and also started doing sessions on guitar and bass in Ohio. They were mostly local jingles and a few gospel records. I was using a Gibson EB-1, a Danelectro 6-string bass, and my P-Bass. I also recorded in Cleveland and Pittsburgh in 1968–72. I was playing guitar in a local band that was pretty good, and a guy from Pittsburgh came to check us out and brought a producer from New York. I happened to be noodling on the bass when the producer was in the room, and he told me I should play bass on sessions. I told him I had done a few, so he flew me up to New York to record with one of his artists. On the session I got to play with Elliot Randall, Richard Crooks, and some other really great players. It freaked me out because all of a sudden I was in this amazing environment.

I went back to Ohio and joined a group called the Jaggerz, who had a hit called "The Rapper." I worked a lot with them in Pittsburgh doing demos on guitar and bass. Then I started playing bass in jazz trios again and doing local jingles.

A friend of mine was doing really well in L.A. playing bass; he called me and said he was so busy he was turning down work and that I should come out there. So I slept on his floor and took some of his overflow. I met a lot of people. This was 1976–79, when things really started rolling for me. I started learning what you had to do in the studio as far as being consistent and developing a tune. I was working with great players doing jingles and movie soundtracks. That's when the education really kicked in.

■ *Was there a producer in L.A. who used you a lot?*

Jerry Fuller. He also got me a writing deal with a publisher. I was doing gigs with Harry Middlebrooks, and I met a lot of actors through him, and I worked for Tommy Oliver and Kelly Gordon. I also did a lot of sessions in the middle of the night for adult movies; they're kind of the equivalent of the Nashville "scab" session. I was doing gigs at night and sessions during the day, and I was doing some writing too.

■ *Did you practice much?*

Not as much as I should have. Usually I would work on things that gave me trouble. I sat down and learned to play some funk bass when I moved to Nashville; I had to make up for lost time on the thumb thing.

■ *What technical matters became more important when you started playing sessions?*

Consistency, touch, accuracy, and playing with the drummer. Also paying attention to what's going on and trying to make something of the song—thinking intelligently when playing a song from beginning to end. I became aware of that pretty quickly. Even when playing the simplest song with just whole-notes, make sure that they're very good whole-notes!

■ *Why did you move to Nashville?*

I was overwhelmed by the size of L.A., and I didn't like being so far away from my family. I had some friends from Ohio who were living in Nashville at the time. They were doing great, and they said I should move there. I told Jerry Fuller I was thinking about moving, so he took me to Nashville with him on a production trip to get some material for Bobby Goldsboro. Jerry introduced me to a lot of people on Music Row, so when I moved to Nashville in 1979 I went right to work.

I did 14 master and demo sessions the first month I was here, which was pretty good for just breaking in. A keyboard player, John Hobbs, gave me a few pointers about playing country music and doing unison parts with the piano. In Nashville the drums, bass, and the left hand of the piano work together, and you need to be aware of the rules. Knowing the Number System is also important.

The first year I didn't make much money. I had my publishing deal that paid me $200 a week, and that helped me get by. By the second year I had started playing on Alabama's albums, and I started getting busy recording with K. T. Oslin, Vern Gosdin, Mel Tillis, and others. I've been rockin' ever since.

I've been doing TV work for the last three years, which has cut down on my session work because some people think I'm not available. So I let them know I can sub the show. I tape *Prime Time Country* from 1:45 to 7:00 p.m., so I can do morning sessions. Sometimes I'll get done taping the show at 6:30, and I'll roar down the road to a session that starts at 7:00.

■ *How much demo work are you doing?*

I do several a week, almost every morning. On some I'm the leader; I sit with the artist and write the charts for the session, and I get to hire my friends. I do as many demos as I can because they're often the most fun. Master sessions are sometimes not as creative because some producers get married to the parts on demos.

■ *Do you ever copy what's been played on a demo when tracking the record?*

It depends. If the producer says he wants what was played on the demo, I will. More often than not I try to capture the demo's spirit. If the demo part is too uncomfortable for me, I try as nicely as I can to guide people away from it. I've also been on records where I played on the demo, so I ended up copying myself!

■ *Do you ever get called in to re-record a part that's already on tape?*

Yes, but it's usually not because someone did a bad job. It just might not be what the producer had in mind. Sometimes there are technical problems with a bass, and the original player might be too busy to come back and fix it.

■ *What do you bring to a session?*

My coffin contains a Danelectro longhorn 6-string, a Jerry Jones longhorn, a G&L 2000 4-string, a Peavey TL-5 with EMG pickups and EQ, a Steinberger 4-string, a Kramer-Ferrington acoustic bass guitar with flatwounds for upright sounds, a Triggs custom 5-string, a Steinberger fretless, a Washburn 5-string acoustic bass, a '57 P-Bass, a 5-string Jazz Bass with a 2TEK bridge and EMGs, and Fender Showman amp with a 15-inch speaker. For strings I use D'Addario, R. Cocco, Fender, and SIT .045-.105s for most basses. For funky things I have a G&L bass that has .030s. On my 5-strings I use .045-.120s. I change strings when they start to sound dull. I tend to play pretty hard, so I have to set my action a little high.

■ *Do you play through a rack system?*

For a while I was using a Mo West preamp and an old Alembic tube preamp that I still play through sometimes, but I've never really used a rack because most studios have great gear. For the TV show I used a Trace Elliot preamp for each bass because of the short time between songs. It's their tube/solid-state unit with a blend control and a high-low compressor. I had one modified so it has line level and mike level. That's all I carry for changing my tone.

■ *You play well with a pick. Do you change your bass tone when you use one?*

I lightly mute the strings with the palm of my right hand, which gives you more apparent bottom. I sometimes use the Fender tailpiece that has a foam-rubber mute. I don't use the pick a lot. I like to take time to find the right sound for each song by using a different bass or whatever. But when I do demos there usually isn't time to be selective because they're recorded so quickly.

■ *Do you like to hear the click when tracking?*

It depends. If there's a war going on in the headphones or if there are a lot of whole notes or stops in the song, then I like to hear the click. Otherwise I can take it or leave it. In the headphones I like to hear more bass than I usually get, but I like to hear a little bit of all the instruments, especially the drums. Sometimes, though, you have to just shut up and accept what you're getting.

■ *Where do you like to put the beat?*

I try not to lean either way. If the artist feels that the track is pushing, then I lay it back. I try to play right with the kick drum. In general Nashville bass is a little bit on the back side compared to L.A. The Muscle Shoals guys really put it on the back side.

■ *When work slows down, how do you recharge your batteries?*

I get away from the business. I'll work on my toy trains or do something else that's not music related. Sometimes I'll write songs and play my guitar. There are times I've caught myself stagnating, but I get jolted out of it by hearing someone like Victor Wooten.

■ *Besides playing ability, what makes a successful session bassist?*

You have to be thick-skinned, because sometimes people will insult you. You need to be able to take direction, and you need to be creative and offer ideas that might be refused. You've got to get along with everybody.

Track 7

In the style of Larry Paxton

Swing eights

♩ = 100

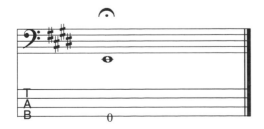

Courtesy Of Larry Paxton
Used By Permission

Dave Pomeroy

"If I get pigeonholed, I hope it's for being a versatile player."

Selected Discography

With Trisha Yearwood: *Hearts in Armor*, *The Song Remembers When*, MCA. With Collin Raye: *In This Life*, Epic. With Emmylou Harris: *Bluebird*, Reprise. With Keith Whitley: *Greatest Hits*, RCA. With Alison Krauss: *I've Got That Old Feeling*, Rounder. With the Chieftains: *Another Country*, RCA. With Tone Patrol: *Thin Air*, Earwave. Solo: *Basses Loaded*, Earwave.

Biography

An in-demand Nashville studio hand, Dave Pomeroy is a tireless promoter of all things bass. He's the driving force behind the annual Basses Loaded all-bass concerts—which features his All Bass Orchestra—and he's recorded a solo CD called *Basses Loaded*. Pomeroy has done sessions with Adrian Belew, Trisha Yearwood, Emmylou Harris, Chet Atkins, Alison Krauss, and Maura

O'Connell, and his Off the Deep End column appears in *Bass Player* magazine.

■ *How did you start playing bass?*

When I was 9 years old I started taking piano lessons and playing clarinet. Then when I was about 10 I started playing string bass in the school orchestra. I played that for a couple of years and switched to electric bass when I was 13 and rock & roll was in full flower.

■ *How important has your orchestral training been?*

It hasn't had much effect, I guess because I landed in Nashville, where so much of the music isn't based on standard notation. I probably get three or four reading calls a year. The early training in orchestral and band music has influenced me in a broader sense, but I've mainly worked with songwriters and artists whose music doesn't need to be translated into that form.

■ *What were those reading sessions?*

I've done a couple of things for Owen Bradley. He recorded piano, bass, and drums and overdubbed synthesizers, and he orchestrated the tracks. The bass lines he wrote out were very simple. I also did a movie-soundtrack session for Janis Ian. She had a very specific idea that was written out. Then in my All Bass Orchestra there are certain parts that are notated. But I'm more of a feel, groove, and melodic player than a great sight-reader. If I got a call for a real heavy reading gig, I would probably defer to someone who does that very well.

■ *What was your first electric bass?*

It was a Kingston, which was like a Kay bass guitar. It had a short-scale neck. I also had a little amp called a Checkmate.

■ *What were the first things you played?*

I learned a couple of licks from "Sunshine of Your Love" and some other things. I had been first chair in the orchestra at one point, so I knew a little bit about the bass. My formal training didn't seem to have much relevance in rock & roll, though. The songs were made up of riffs and chord progressions, so I just started learning riffs and chords. I played along with records endlessly. I had a couple of friends who were also trying to play, so as soon as we knew a song we would put together whatever instrumentation we had and try to make primitive recordings. My senior year I was in a band that actually worked. I had already been accepted at a college, so my parents went along with it as long as I didn't miss any school. It took a while before I was actually making a living at it, and even then I wasn't making a lot.

■ *Did you know early on you wanted a career as a bass player?*

I knew instantly when I played the electric bass for the first time. I just loved doing it. I pursued it because it was really fun and I enjoyed performing. But I never really thought in terms of becoming a session musician. I wanted to be in a successful band like the Beatles. I left college after a couple of years because I wasn't studying what I wanted to study. My parents were stationed in Belgium, so I took my bass and amp over with me and decided I wanted to go to London and play rock & roll. My parents were shocked, but they eventually got over it.

I was 20 when I went to London, and that was my introduction to the real world of the music business. I moved there knowing one person—whom I had met only once—but in three days I got a job playing with an American-style cover band. That ended up being my angle to get a work permit—that I was bringing something uniquely American to thc band that wasn't going to put any English bass player out of work. I stayed for a year and played in a few bands. I learned that if I wanted to make it, it would be important to be in a major music center.

At that point a friend had just moved to Nashville and gotten a publishing deal, and she asked me to play on her record. The record session never panned out, but it got me to Nashville. That was 19 years ago, and I've been here ever since.

■ *Is it important to get your chops up before moving to a city like Nashville, Los Angeles, or New York?*

The most I feel I've ever learned is when I've gotten myself in a situation that's almost over my head. There's no substitute for being there with the big guys. If you feel a particular music center is right for you, then go there—and start waiting! You've got to be prepared to pay your dues. The goods news is, these days there are more tools available to prepare you for what you'll have to do.

■ *Some people think Nashville is just country music.*

That's only one color in the rainbow, and I get annoyed with the stereotype. I chuckle when people book me for a date and warn me it's not a country project. It's perfectly fine with me if it's not! Stereotypes also put players in a box. Most of the good musicians here can play anything. There are incredible rock & roll, pop, and jazz players, and

there's a Christian music scene, too. Of course I love good country music. I workcd for Don Williams for 14 ycars, and he has been a huge influence in almost everything I do. But most of all, this is a town full of great songwriters of all descriptions.

■ *When you first came to Nashville did you plan to do sessions?*

Not really. I don't think I knew exactly what a session player was or was supposed to do. I loved reading album credits and was aware that the same players seemed to play on certain records, but I just wanted to work and be heard.

My first job here was a road gig with Sleepy La Beef, a rockabilly artist who knows a million songs. He never rehearses; he plays stream-of-consciousness style and you just follow. I didn't truly understand country, gospel, authentic blues, or roots music then, so I learned a lot from him.

After that I got a couple of sessions, but I still didn't fully understand what was expected of me. On one of my first sessions the drummer was Freddy Fletcher, Willie Nelson's nephew, and Freddy asked me if I'd be interested in playing with Guy Clark. So I started going out of town a little bit with Guy, who was also sharing the band with Billy Joe Shaver, so I started doing gigs with both of them. I kept meeting people, which is what it's all about, and got called to do a session for Steve Young, another good songwriter. That was a "spec" session—you "expect" to get paid for it someday! They were using number charts, which I didn't completely understand, so I wrote out my own chord chart; I remember getting looks from the other guys. Six months later I got a check in the mail. I went to the music store and saw my name on the album, and I thought, "God, I'm on a record!"

A little later I got a shot at the Don Williams gig, and playing with him really got me started in Nashville. He was one of the few artists who actually promoted his band, and he helped us get a record deal. We did a pretty eclectic album that didn't make it in the country world, so we split up.

I kept playing with other people and started pursuing demos. I figured out that studio work was the thing to do, but I still didn't know how to get there. I tried meeting different songwriters and did a lot of sessions for free. My big break was in 1985. Joe Allen, who played bass on all of Don's records, was out of town, so Don and Garth Fundis, his co-producer, asked me to play on the next record. I met Kenny Malone, who was the drummer on the dates, and we instantly bonded. That album had a couple of No. 1 singles; it was a big deal for me to play on it.

In 1987 Don left the road for a year, and Garth Fundis was starting to spread his wings as a producer. He asked me to play on a record for a singer named Keith Whitley, and it was absolutely magic. It also yielded three No. 1 singles. That was when my electric upright bass really came into play. That long slide on Keith's "I'm No Stranger to the Rain" put me on the map. I approached the bass with a string bass vibe in mind—not a Jaco approach—and it seemed to

work with Keith's voice. I played the electric upright on all but one track of that album.

■ *How did you get started on that instrument?*

In London I had seen Eberhard Weber leading a band and playing an electric upright. I loved the sound and I started buying his records. A while later I saw a Harry Fleishman electric upright advertised in *Guitar Player* magazine. So I called Harry, and he brought one to my hotel when I was playing with Don Williams near Denver. I fell in love with it and felt I could do something cool with it. I ordered a 5-string with a low *B*, which in 1981 was definitely ahead of its time. Don lent me half the money. When it came I sounded terrible on it because I hadn't played upright in a long time. I got so frustrated I put it in the case for two weeks, but then I finally decided I was going to learn to play it no matter what. I had five years under my belt when I did Keith Whitley's record.

About half my work now is on electric upright. My bag is sound. I have 18 basses, and I use 12 of them a lot. If I get pigeonholed, I hope it's for being a versatile player.

■ *On the electric upright what kind of action and pickups do you use?*

I generally play with pretty high action—I think string tension is a big part of tone. The electric upright, which has a $36\frac{1}{2}$-inch scale, is set up a little easier than a string bass. The pickup layout has been modified over the years. It now has five pickups: a huge

double-coil, a Barcus-Berry piezo under the bridge, an EMG-P by the fingerboard, an Underwood on the bridge, and a Bartolini magnetic five-piece electric upright pickup mounted between the double-coil and the bridge. The different outputs are fed into a mixer, and the Underwood goes through an Ampeg SVT preamp to fatten up the tone. I use heavy-gauge GHS Brite Flats, and I change them every January!

■ *Any advice for aspiring session bassists?*

You need to be hard on yourself, at least in the early going. It's very easy to get complacent. I never forget there are thousands of people who would love to be doing what I'm doing. You've got to question yourself and make sure you've got the desire to stick it out. If you really feel like you're willing to make the commitment, then you need to figure out what city is going to make sense for you.

It's important to trust your instincts and follow your heart. I've abandoned ideas because nobody else seemed to understand them, and then five or ten years down the line I've seen someone have success with the same musical concept. So you've got to listen to your own voice and do what you feel is best.

Basses Loaded *and the benefit CD* Blue Christmas *are available from Earwave Records, Box 40857, Nashville, TN 37204. The concert video* The Day the Bass Players Took Over the World *is available through* Bass Player.

In the style of Dave Pomeroy
"Not Forgotten"

By Dave Pomeroy

Track 8

♩ = 99

Leland Sklar

"I'm amazed at how bad a bass can sound soloed but how rich and beautiful it sounds with the other instruments."

Selected Discography

With Jackson Browne: *Running on Empty*, *The Pretender*, Asylum. With Linda Ronstadt: *Cry Like a Rainstorm—Howl Like the Wind*, Elektra. With Phil Collins: *No Jacket Required*, *Serious Hits … Live*, Atlantic. With Marty Stuart: *Hillbilly Rock*, MCA. With Billy Cobham: *Spectrum*, Atlantic. With James Taylor: *Never Die Young*, *Flag*, Columbia; *Gorilla*, *One Man Dog*, *Mud Slide Slim & the Blue Horizon*, Warner Bros.

Biography

Leland Sklar's ability to adapt to any situation has garnered him respect in many genres and made him one of the most sought-after session bassists in pop, rock, and country since the 1970s. A truly worldwide artist, his extensive résumé includes work with Phil

Collins, James Taylor, Vince Gill, Billy Cobham, George Strait, Hall & Oates, Jackson Brown, Ricky Skaggs, and Linda Ronstadt.

■ *How did you get started on bass?*

I started studying piano when I was 5, and when I was 12 I changed to string bass because they had no string bass players in junior high. The music teacher, Ted Lynn, taught me how to play, and I fell in love with the whole psychology of the instrument.

When I started playing electric bass, I would learn songs off of albums, and rather than just playing them at 33 RPM, I would bump the speed up to 45 RPM and play along. Once I got real comfortable playing faster, I would slow it back down to 33 RPM. That opened up a different world of responding to the material, because I knew exactly where it was headed at a different tempo. That allowed me to improvise and be a little more expressive.

■ *How did you establish yourself before your first sessions?*

I was playing around clubs in L.A., which at that time had a very active scene. There were clubs you could walk into with your instrument and sit in. I met a lot of great people, from the guys in Chicago to Jimi Hendrix. I think performance is an essential part of the process—I would still rather play live than do studio work—and I went into that scene with no aspirations. I was hoping to make it by playing in a band.

■ *What was your first studio experience?*

It was with a band called Wolfgang in the late '60s—the group broke up before our album got finished. After that was probably the beginnings of James Taylor's recordings. James and I met through Wolfgang, and I started recording with him. My first "legit" session was with James.

When session work started, I had no concept of what the process was or what was involved with being a studio musician. At that time Joe Osborn and Carol Kaye were the dominant studio bassists in Los Angeles. Bobby West and others were on the scene, but Carol was pretty much the founding rock. In 1967 I was in a band called Group Therapy that was produced by Mike Post [a major L.A. TV

and film music writer and producer]. We were just young kids, so the record company didn't want us to play on the record—we just did the vocals. They called in professional players, and we got to watch the session. It was Earl Palmer on drums, Carol Kaye on bass, Michele Rubini, Michael Melvoin, and Larry Knechtel on keyboards, Jim Gordon on percussion, and Dennis Budimir on guitar. I ended up becoming close friends with those people and working alongside them. But back then I just watched and was amazed by the whole process. I was used to dragging my gear around in my car and setting up in a club and playing, hoping I wouldn't get ripped off at the end of the night.

■ *You eventually became Mike Post's first-call bassist.*

Mike said later on that he thought that of all the guys in the band, I would be the one who had a good shot at doing what I ended up doing. We had stayed friends through that period, and as he became aware of how my career was evolving, it seemed logical to work together. The first thing I did was *The Rockford Files*, which was early in his career, too. I was thrilled to be working with him.

■ *Did any bass players guide you?*

I would have to say no. There were a lot of guys I heard on records, from Bob Moseley with Moby Grape to McCartney to Jack Bruce to Roy Estrada from the original Mothers of Invention. But the session scene happened so fast that I wasn't even aware of who the studio players were. I had to make my own way, and I was completely naive about the process, even down to what to bring and how to deal with charts. It still happens. When I started going to Nashville I suddenly had to read number charts, and I was in the middle of a whole new ball game.

■ *Do you practice scales?*

They're probably very important, but to be honest I really suck at running scales. I enjoy just sitting and playing, but I don't necessarily do it from a practice standpoint. I've evolved my style around a lot of my limitations. I've had a lot of hand injuries—tendon problems and deep cuts because I like to work with machinery—and I don't have a lot of dexterity in the second and third fingers of my left hand. So a lot of my playing is with my first and fourth fingers. I have a different approach of getting to places than a lot of players I know; I've built my style around slides and glisses between notes.

I don't feel I'm a real proficient player technically, but I know how to use the instrument to my best advantage. There are different wells you can draw from. If I want to play fretless bass, I think about Pino Palladino because I admire his fretless playing. On string bass I'll think about Edgar Meyer.

The better you are technically, the freer you are to be expressive. You have to practice until your chops become secondary, so that when an idea hits you you're not trying to figure out *how* to play it—you're just responding emotionally in your playing. Sometimes I'll listen to things I did 20 years ago, and I realize I would never play that way

now. On some things I completely overplayed; I don't think I was responding to the music in the best way possible.

■ *Is it important to practice with a metronome or drum machine?*

It's crucial! Your job description as a rhythm-section musician is rhythm. I work with a lot of artists who have spent their entire lives sitting at home playing the piano and singing. Your job is to harness them to make a pop record, and you have to have confidence in your time. That's not to say you don't respond emotionally and allow the time to move. When I work with great drummers like Russ Kunkel or Carlos Vega, the time generally moves around. That's because we're responding emotionally to the music and doing what feels natural. Recording with drum machines doesn't allow me the freedom to be as expressive as I would like to be. But everyone should have a metronome or drum machine when they practice.

Often when I'm cutting with a click track, I'll turn the click off in my headphones and just listen to the drummer so I can work around him rather than play to the click. That allows my part to feel a bit looser.

■ *Do you ever find yourself pushing when the drummer is dragging?*

I can lean on drummers pretty hard if I think they're dragging—I'll pull the drummer along. But I don't like to do that because it makes me play in a slightly different way and not give my best performance. Sometimes I'll say to the drummer, "This is kind of dragging—can we focus on it a little more and see what's going on?"

I work with the whole gamut of players, from those who are a lot older than me to players in their early 20s who might be intimidated. The first thing to do is try to develop a rapport so everyone will feel as comfortable and upbeat as possible. It's a serious business with a lot of money being spent and careers on the line, but it should be fun. I try to keep a light-hearted mood and B.S. with a new drummer a little bit so we're both comfortable. That way if things aren't locking in, we'll feel comfortable talking about it.

■ *There are times when a drummer just isn't capable of playing well.*

When that happens I just do the best I can and get out of there. It's like building a house: You might be a brilliant plumber, but if the electrician is doing a shoddy job there's nothing you can do about it. You just hope the place doesn't burn down after you finish!

■ *What about players who refuse to play what they're asked?*

If I were the producer, I would fire that player on the spot. When people request that you play something, you should at least try it. The first time or two I'll play exactly what they want to hear and then suggest an idea. But you absolutely owe it to them to play what they're looking for even if you don't like it. It's your job to make them happy— not theirs to make you happy. The only time they make you happy is when they order lunch in a timely fashion and pick up the check.

■ *What bass works best for you in the studio?*

The bass I've use for the past 20 years is sort of a Fender hybrid. It's one of the very first Charvel bodies—a blank alder Precision-shaped piece—and a really good Precision neck I had reshaped like a '62 Jazz neck because I don't like the P-Bass shape. When I was in the shop I saw mandolin fretwire hanging on the wall, and I said, "Let's put that in this thing instead of jumbo or medium frets." The guys said, "Are you kidding?" Since then I've had mandolin frets put in every bass I've had. You get all of the accuracy of jumbo frets, but if you lighten your touch slightly you can create sounds that are very similar to fretless. They're also very easy to play. I've played this bass every day for 20 years, and I've had only three refrets. I have a strong hand and I play really hard, so they obviously hold up.

The bass has first-generation EMG pickups, but I put the Precision configuration where the Jazz pickups would be and reversed their position, so the low-string pickup is closer to the bridge. I figured the *E* and the *A* strings could use a little more clarity, and it really evened out the sound. The EMGs are active; they run on 18 volts with two volumes and a tone control like a Fender. The bridge is an old Badass.

One of my most essential pieces of equipment is a Hipshot *D*-tuner. I've got 5- and 6-string basses, but in my heart I'm a 4-string player—in electric music there's a wonderful tonal melding of 4-string bass and guitar. But on 5-string guys tend to play too low, creating a sonic hole between the bass and the guitar.

■ *How do you set pickup height in relation to the strings?*

Usually not too close and not too deep in the body. I like having them high enough to be able to rest my thumb on the pickup edge. I play hard and get a lot of string movement, so I like them set so they don't come in contact with the strings. Most players are appalled by my action. They can't believe someone would play a bass with action that high.

I tried playing one of John Entwistle's basses, and I could not make a sound come out of it—the action was so low you could barely put a piece of paper between the strings and the frets. Then he picked it up and blew my mind. On my bass you can put the whole tablet between them!

■ *Do you put on fresh strings for each session?*

No. On the road if I'm working a lot, I'll change strings once a week. In the studio I pretty much do it by ear. If it starts sounding a little dull, then I'll change them, but that might be every couple of months.

■ *Do you get a stronger fundamental from a more settled string?*

Not necessarily. I tend to change strings when I notice the top end disappearing. I also keep a very close eye on my batteries. With my 4-string's older EMGs I can go through two 9-volts a week.

I carry a tester with me; I usually change a battery when it gets down to 8.4 volts. It really makes a difference in the sound when they drop off a little bit.

A company in England made 9-volts that were actually 10.7, and they were great.

■ *What gear do you take to a session?*

I bring a trunk with my 4-string, a Dingwall 5-string, a Yamaha TRB5 fretless, a Washburn AB40 acoustic bass guitar, a Washburn AB45 fretless acoustic bass guitar for upright sounds, a Yamaha piccolo bass, a Tube Works DI, a Boss octave divider, a T.C. Electronic chorus/flanger, a tuner, and extra strings. The DI is a real simple system that's mike level, not line level, so it usually requires a Neve preamp or other mike pre. I usually leave that up to the engineer.

I use the Boss octave divider on a lot of things. Sometimes I double parts using the octave splitter or double my bass part using the piccolo bass. But 90 percent of what I do involves using just the 4-string through the DI. If I'm doing a big project in Nashville I'll try to coerce them into letting me ship a trunk there. But usually I just carry a 4-string and a 5-string on the plane in a double gig bag.

On a record the most important thing is to keep the bass as clean and pure as possible. Guitar players seem to be incapable of playing without delay or some kind of crap, and when you have delay and chorus on keyboards and effects on drums, a clean bass gives you good sonic stability. Also, if you commit altered tones to tape too early, there's nothing they can do about it later. It may not be the right thing by the time they put on strings or background vocals.

■ *Some producers expect the recorded bass part to stand up well by itself.*

I feel the same way, except I can't stand to listen to my bass soloed. I'm amazed at how bad a bass can sound soloed but how rich and beautiful it sounds with the other instruments. And I can't dictate what bass would sound best for you. Abe Laboriel's got basses that are so funky they're almost hysterical, but when he plays them they sound great.

■ *Do you ever mike an amp in the studio?*

Hardly ever, because my 4-string sounds so good—most engineers are blown away when they hear it. But I sometimes use an amp because I don't care for bass in headphones—I would rather feel the sound of an amp.

■ *What do you like to hear in your headphones?*

I like to hear as close to a final mix as I can, so I'll have an idea how it's ultimately going to sound. I also like the singer to be there so it becomes a song instead of just reading a chart. A good cue system allows you to respond to everything instead of just bits and pieces, but usually headphones are the weakest link in any studio experience.

■ *Do you try to adapt the console to fit your sound?*

Never. I give them my sound and let them deal with it. Each engineer does his own thing, and every studio has its own sound. Sometimes I'll hear sounds in the studio that I'll hate, but the engineer will say, "I know this room very well, so don't let this sound deceive you—it's going down great." Then I'll

hear the record and realize he was right.

I try to express as much confidence in the engineer as I can. The only thing I hate is when the engineer runs my bass into a limiter or compressor before I've played the first note. It's like salting your meal before you've tasted it. The dynamics of my playing are in my hands, and I don't like being limited except to catch radical peaks. It really bugs me when the compression makes it so I'm hearing the same level whether I'm playing hard or soft.

■ *You have a way of using sustained notes to make a track flow.*

I don't think about it. I'm just responding emotionally. On Vince Gill's ballads, for instance, some of the bars contain just whole- or half-notes, so I need to create a pad so he can soar on top.

Sometimes I use a really light vibrato, and that helps the note sustain. I focus on where the downbeat actually hits more than when I clip off the note. It's a style of bass playing a lot of people talk to me about, but I don't really hear it when it's happening. When I play it's sort of an out-of-body experience—the last thing I'm listening to is me.

It can be a lot harder to play a whole-note than to play a bunch of 32nd-notes. If your only note in a bar is a whole-note, then you had better make it a good one.

■ *How should players present themselves professionally?*

The most important thing is promptness and attention. If I'm told the session is a 12 o'clock downbeat, I'm there at 20 minutes till 12, set up, tuned, and

ready to play. There's a lot of money and energy going into this thing, and you can't be lax about it. When you're at the session, pay attention and don't noodle around—that can be distracting.

The minute some players are done with the take, they're on the phone or doing some other thing. But I think it's important to be involved. Your name is going to appear on the record, and you want to be proud of it. When the playbacks come around, go in and listen and make suggestions if you have any.

When I go to a session I still treat it like the first day of my career, and I put 150 percent into it. Sometimes it's frustrating, but other times it's the most fantastic thing you've ever experienced.

Track 9

In the style of Lee Sklar
"It Hurts Me Too"

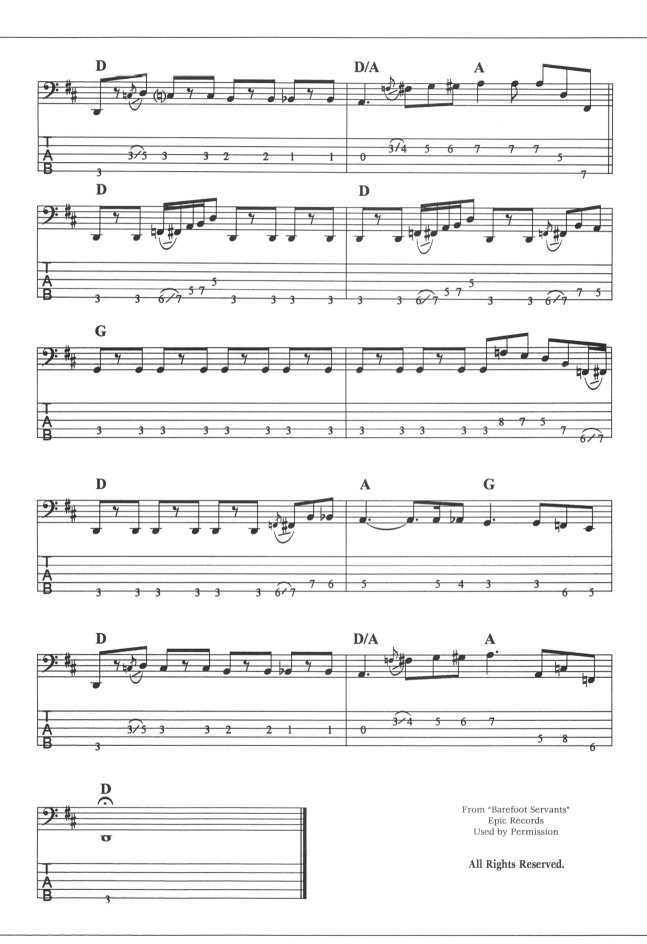

From "Barefoot Servants"
Epic Records
Used by Permission

Neil Stubenhaus

"When I walk into a date I give them everything I possibly can. When I leave I want to be sure they're thrilled."

Selected Discography

With Quincy Jones: *Back on the Block*, *Q's Jook Joint*, Qwest. With Don Henley: *Actual Miles*, Geffen. With Michael Bolton: *Soul Provider*, Columbia. With John Fogerty: *Eye of the Zombie*, Warner Bros. With Tom Scott: *Streamlines*, *Flashpoint*, GRP. With Take 6: *Join the Band*, Reprise. With Gino Vannelli: *Night Walker*, Arista. With Rickie Lee Jones: *Flying Cowboys*, Geffen. With Rod Stewart: *Vagabond Heart*, Warner Bros. With Billy Joel: *The Bridge*, Columbia.

Biography

A top L.A. session bassist for many years, Neil Stubenhaus has played for a who's-who of record-date clients ranging from Quincy Jones, Barbra Streisand, and Frank Sinatra to Joe Cocker, Don Henley, and Natalie Cole. He's also done numerous movie soundtracks,

including *Hercules*, *Men in Black*, *Speed II*, *Mars Attack*, and *Sleepers*.

■ *How did you get started playing the bass?*

I started on drums and then played guitar, but I found out there weren't many good bass players around. When I was 15 I bought a fretless Hofner from a friend, but couple of days later I realized the neck was warped. So I went to Manny's in New York City and bought a Fender P-Bass.

I thought about bass all the time and learned everything I could about it. I picked up things from other players around town I admired, and I learned lines off records.

■ *When did you start recording?*

Early on in Connecticut I did a lot of recording with bands I was in. When I got to Boston I was called by some ex-members of the Young Rascals to do some recording with one of their producers. I was using a Jazz Bass in those days.

The more serious sessions came in 1978 when I moved to L.A. I was working in Larry Carlton's band, and he turned me on to a few jingles, which was good experience. I was ready to do whatever came along, and session work definitely appealed to me. I've always felt that setting your sights on one thing is a mistake. I never thought like that. I followed whatever opportunity came along.

There were a lot of bassists working then, and I looked up to most of them— Abraham Laboriel, Lee Sklar, David Hungate.

■ *Were you still using your Jazz Bass?*

Yes, but I think I had replaced the neck pickup with a P-bass pickup. It gave it a fatter sound.

■ *Were the older players hard on you in the beginning?*

No, everybody was very supportive. The music business was a lot more secure back then. Now there aren't a lot of younger players breaking in, because there's not as much work to spread around. People stick with known players, and it's the same people now as it was back then. Back then the crowd was in their 20s, and now they're in their 40s. That pretty much tells the story.

There's a whole other circuit of players making a name for themselves now doing rock & roll projects. But they wouldn't be able to walk into a movie date and cut a track in just three hours.

■ *You're following in the footsteps of Chuck Domanico, who does a lot of movie and TV soundtracks.*

Chuck was one of the most popular upright and electric bassists in film work, and he's still very busy, mostly on upright bass. He's the best upright player in town, so he deserves all that work.

When I started doing sessions, TV shows used orchestras, and everyone was doing as much TV as they were records. There isn't much TV work anymore. I do maybe 40 dates a year for sitcoms like *Wings*, *Step by Step*, and *Murphy Brown*, usually the themes and little cues.

■ *Are the people who hire you usually aware you're a double- or triple-scale player?*

Most of the time I don't have to bring it up. The fact that scales are established makes it less confrontational. But some people don't know anything about it. There are foreign artists and producers who come to town and ask a few questions, and they learn quickly.

■ *What's your approach to playing
a session?*

There is no single mind-set; it's a game of personalities. Whoever I'm working for, I find out what they want and work toward that. Usually it's music I know instinctively, so I know what to do. I just try to perfect it. When I walk into a date I give them everything I possibly can. When I leave I want to be sure they're thrilled. I want them to listen to the tape and call me back a few days later and say, "It's great." You want to please everybody all the way to the ceiling.

■ *Is it important to play exactly what
you're asked to play?*

Sometimes when people tell you what to play they are absolute, and they know what they want. Some might tell you they know what they want but will change their minds if they hear something new. So it's important to play what you're asked to play, but you should also offer options.

■ *What about players who don't want
to alter their approach?*

That's often valid, because ideally you hire a person for what that person does best. You have to respect that artistry. I'm more flexible than that, but when I walk into a session, I would rather play it the way I hear it, and 99 percent of the time that's exactly what they want me to do. I can't think of a movie composer who would want me to stick to something specifically. They usually want me to put my spin on it so it sounds natural and makes things work. I try to be as flexible and as versatile as possible.

I come from a kind of acrobatic musical background. When I was younger I liked to play a lot and experiment and be self-indulgent. But music needs to be tasteful. If a bass player is bent on playing for himself, they're either going to tell him to stop or replace his part. Sometimes they may call a flashy guy and tell him to go for it, but he still has to make it work for the track.

■ *Does a session bassist have to be easy
to get along with to be successful?*

Absolutely. But then again, if your musicianship can make or break a record, it may not be so important whether you're such a great person. However, being easy to work with holds a lot of weight.

■ *What basses do you bring to a typical
session?*

I bring a James Tyler 4-string, a Tyler fretted 5, a Pedulla fretless 5, a Washburn AB45 5-string acoustic bass guitar, and a Peavey CyberBass MIDI bass. I use Rotosound Swing Bass strings, gauges .045-.105. On the *B* string I've gone back and forth from .125 to .130, but I currently prefer .130. I like my action comfortable but high enough not to buzz.

Most of my basses have Seymour Duncan pickups and all have active electronics, although I don't always use the preamps. I also bring an SWR Redhead amplifier to sessions. It has built-in direct box; I added a custom one that's passive and has a Jensen transformer. The SWR also has three processors built into it: a compressor, an SWR Mr. Tone Controls equalizer, and a Yamaha SPX900. I use it for a pitch-shift effect like the Eventide Harmonizer. I also bring a MIDI synth rack for the Peavey CyberBass, which includes a Mini Moog and some samplers. I like the amp to be right next to me because it gives me more control. I can adjust the preamp, which affects the sound going to the direct box. The rack and everything else is right there.

■ *What EQ points work well with your basses?*

It changes from session to session. If it sounds a little dull, I'll bring up a little 500Hz. It's subtle. I stay away from boosting the top end. I leave that to the engineer, who has a better perspective.

■ *Do you prefer to have a miked amp on every session?*

No, I prefer not to because it slows things down and clouds things up a bit. The direct track doesn't really mix that well with the amp track. Some engineers who do it all the time know how to blend it, and if they want to I'll let them.

■ *Where do you like to put the beat?*

In general I play on the beat, but it depends on the song. Sometimes I like to lay it back a little bit, but I never want it to sound rushed.

Basically, if the drummer is bad you're in trouble, and if the drummer is good you're okay. I might be with a drummer who doesn't have the concept of a slow ballad. After four or five tries I'll either tell somebody else what to play or tell them what's wrong with the

track and how to fix it. If it's just the drummer, I'll tell them to work with the guy and get a drum track, and when they're done I'll put the bass part on. You have to be very diplomatic, but it usually works.

■ *If the singer's rushing and you're playing to a click track, what do you prefer to hear in the mix?*

When that happens the musicians all look at one another, and almost immediately someone yells to the engineer to take the vocal down. A lot of studios now have little boxes that sit next to each musician so you can adjust your own mix. That's ideal.

■ *Do you listen to the click plus the drummer or just the drummer?*

I listen to both the click and drummer. I've never really practiced with a click, but I became comfortable with it as I did more sessions.

For that matter, I never practiced much on my technique, either. Not that I shouldn't have, but I didn't. Electric bass doesn't require a specific technique. There are rights and wrongs on upright bass, but electric allows for a wide variety of techniques.

■ *How much of your finger do you pluck with?*

I put some meat into it. I modeled a lot my playing after Michael Henderson. I used to watch him play with Miles Davis—he knocked me out. There was a lot of emotion to the way he attacked the strings, and he put a lot of finger into it.

■ *Where do you position your plucking hand?*

Between the two pickups, not way back by the bridge.

■ *Do you alter note length for certain tracks?*

It depends what they want in the track. Sometimes they want it longer than I hear it, so I'll make it longer. But it's not something I think about while I'm playing. It's instinctive. In a ballad, for example, my notes are almost all connected. The decay that occurs naturally with electric bass is enough.

■ *Do you feel you've lost a youthful, uninhibited type of playing as you've gotten older?*

No, I don't at all. I'm the same way I was 20 years ago except without the drugs. I play everything I want to play. The most uninhibited playing is usually the first run-through. If I have to edit it for the final product, I do. Times have changed and musical styles have changed, but I don't enjoy it any less. And the better the musical content, the more you will be inspired to play something brilliant.

■ *Any advice for aspiring studio bassists?*

You need to have great instincts about music and people. There is a delicate balance. You have to know what to play and when to play it. You have to be able to judge when to agree and when not to agree.

You also have to fit in and be natural. People will sense it if you're trying too hard. Don't act like a kid in a candy store. You have to feel equal to the people you're surrounded by—you have to have confidence.

Track 10

In the style of Neil Stubenhaus
"Cool Joe, Mean Joe (Killer Joe)"

Music By Benny Golson
Lyrics By Quincy Jones

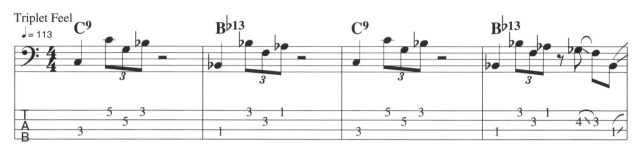

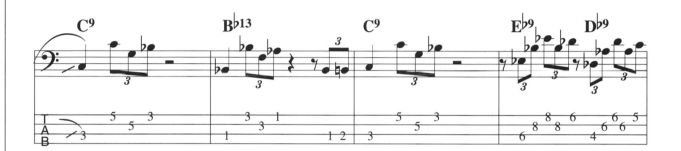

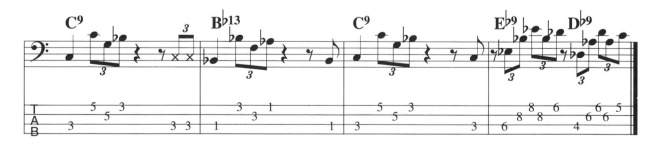

From Quincy Jones' "Q's Jook Joint" - Rap By Queen Latifah
copyright 1995 Time Step Music/Hee Bee Dooinit Music Corp. ASCAP
Adm. by W.B. Music Corp. Used By Permission

Glenn Worf

"You can get carried away with trying to make everything clean and pristine."

Selected Discography

With Mark O'Connor: *Heroes*, *The New Nashville Cats*, Warner Bros. With Mark Knopfler: *Golden Heart*, Warner Bros. With David Ball: *Thinkin' Problem*, Warner Bros. With Pam Tillis: *All of This Love*, Arista. With George Strait: *Easy Come Easy Go*, *Pure Country*, MCA. With Clint Black: *No Time to Kill*, RCA. With Emmylou Harris: *Brand New Dance*, Reprise. With Kevin Welch & the Overtones: *Western Beat*, Reprise. With Mark Collie: *Mark Collie*, MCA.

Biography

Glenn Worf's great tone and his ability to double on electric and upright have made him an invaluable Nashville session hand. His credits include recordings with Mark Knopfler,

David Ball, Marty Stuart, Alan Jackson, Mark O'Connor, George Strait, and Pam Tillis, and Glenn was also the bassist for TNN's *American Music Shop*.

■ *What drew you to the bass?*

When my parents took me to the HemisFair in San Antonio, Texas, in 1968, there was a band playing, and I happened to get a seat right in front of the bass player's amp. Every time he played a note it slapped against my stomach—I could feel the power of the instrument. I was 13 years old and had been playing the guitar for a couple of years, but after that night I decided bass was for me. I got a bass within a few months.

■ *Did you take lessons?*

I mostly fumbled around on my own, just trying to figure out the geography of it. I played along with records and tried to figure out what the bass player was doing. I also watched a couple of bass players. Later on I started tuning in to the more mature players, but I still didn't take lessons. After I graduated from high school I decided to study more seriously, so I went to a music college in my home state of Wisconsin for two-and-a-half years.

When I entered college I had to play a classical instrument. I had no interest in the string bass in the beginning, but it was the obvious choice. After college it was many years before I got back to it.

I played electric bass in the jazz program and string bass in the school orchestra, and I was studying with James Klute, who was the principal bassist of the Minnesota Orchestra. During all this I was also playing steel guitar in country bands, sometimes working five nights a week. When I left school I went on the road and played in clubs, alternating between steel and bass.

When I moved to Nashville in 1979 I found there weren't many steel guitarists working because country music was trying to sound more pop. Plus there were so many great steel players already established. So I committed myself to being a bass player.

■ *I sometimes hear an approach similar to Bob Moore's in your playing.*

I'm delighted and thrilled if you hear that, because the man has been a huge influence. At the time I was listening to him I wasn't playing string bass, but when I played songs he played on, I tried to capture his feel on electric. His sound on string bass was amazing—it was huge. He also had a way of making things swing, even on very traditional songs.

I'm very much into rock & roll and blues, too; I love Willie Dixon's string bass playing. I also listened to Jack Bruce, Paul McCartney, and Lance Hoppen, who played for the band Orleans. He could be real funky and precise at the same time. I've been friends with him for many years.

■ *What bassists did you look up to when you started playing in Nashville?*

I came here during the changing of the guard. Bob Moore was still one main guy and Henry Strezlecki was the other. But a number of other bassists were coming in, mainly David Hungate, Joe Osborn, and Larry Paxton. Those three caught everybody's fancy and became very busy in a short time. That wasn't the case for me.

■ *Did you concentrate on anything to help you improve?*

The only way you get better is to work at the things you don't do well. I spent many hours on the club circuit reading Bach concertos and practicing things I knew I would never be called to do. I also played jazz changes, funk exercises, and so on, even though I wasn't playing jobs in those styles. I always hoped I would become a session bassist, and a working session bassist has to be able to play all styles well.

One of the best skills I learned in college was how to be a student, to discipline yourself to explore things that you can't do. Music is a lifelong pursuit; it doesn't matter how good you get, the next day you start all over. You might want to learn to play with a pick. When that happens I recommend playing with it in as many different circumstances as you can. You can practice muting the strings with the palm of your picking hand while picking, or try string-crossing exercises and scales.

On string bass you can work on blue-grass-style slapping, long-note jazz-style lines, and older swing feels with shorter notes. You should expose yourself to music other than what you do best. You have to experiment and have the courage to make mistakes.

■ *What was your first master session in Nashville?*

It was a disco song, and I was very nervous working with musicians I didn't know. Every note was written out—on the front *and* the back of the page—*and* I was supposed to do a bass solo right at the point where I had to turn the page! The solo was also written out, but it wasn't too complex—a weird octave sort of thing. I turned the page with my right hand while playing hammer-ons with my left, and I was sweating through my shirt. But I acted like it was no big deal, and nobody gave it a second thought.

■ *What basses were you using?*

I came to Nashville with a P-Bass I got in high school and a fretless P-Bass, and I used Rotosound roundwounds.

For years I tried to get people to let me record with the fretless, but they weren't into it.

■ *If you could bring just one bass to all your sessions, which would it be?*

My old Fender P-Bass with EMG pickups. The EMGs have the right amount of bottom end, and I like the highs, though some players think they're too glassy sounding. I play very hard and set my basses with very high action because I like them to fight back a little bit, and EMGs work well for that type of sound.

I also have a couple of old P-Basses with stock pickups, and in the right circumstances nothing sounds better. I also have a stock Music Man that sounds fantastic for certain things.

I discovered that when I added a lot of treble to the bass, I sometimes wouldn't hear it very well in the final mix. Talking to engineers I found that adding too much treble makes the bass compete with higher-register instruments and with the vocals, so the engineers had to turn down the bass. So I started going the other direction, bringing up the bottom end in a way that allowed for a big sound without getting muddy.

■ *How much 5-string work are you doing?*

It depends on the style of music. I have a Sadowsky 5-string with EMGs that I absolutely adore. Roger Sadowsky builds basses that go to tape very well, with a full bottom that's not mushy. When 5-strings first came out it seemed like players camped out on the low *B* string, but I think you need to be careful about that. It's got to be the right time and the right song.

■ *Do you like to track with new strings?*

I'm not big on changing strings all the time. I used to do that a lot, but over the years I've decided I'm not that interested in the top end of the bass— I'm more into the bottom. I think maybe that's allowed me to work because people associate me with having a meaty sound. So I change strings only when they won't do what I need them to do. One of my old P-Basses has flatwounds from the '70s, but on the other P-Bass I use a lot, I change strings every two or three weeks. I use mostly .045-.105 gauge with a .125 or .128 for the *B* string. I use Sadowsky strings on the 5-strings.

■ *You use an SWR Grand Prix tube preamp into a Tube Tech limiter. Why did you change from the older Teletronix LA-2A tube limiter?*

I loved the sound of the LA-2A, but it couldn't catch the fast transients. It's great for ballads and a lot of other things, but on some tracks the notes get right by it. The Tube Tech is a good combination of the sound of an LA-2A and the ability to catch the fast transients. I don't use a lot of compression, but it's nice to have it if I need it.

■ *Why do you put the compressor after the preamp?*

I like to set the sound and EQ with the preamp and then adjust the limiter according to those settings. But it's important to cooperate with the engineer.

I started using a rack because I wasn't getting the sounds that I wanted

to hear. I also have a Telefunken V72 mike pre I sometimes use without an EQ as a DI, and an SWR Mr. Tone Controls EQ that can be patched with the V72 or the Grand Prix if needed. I get the proper +4 recording level with the Grand Prix output straight to the tape machine—which sounds great—or with a combination of the Grand Prix to the Tube Tech and then to tape.

■ *How do you decide what EQ setting to use?*

It depends on the song, the bass, and if I'm playing with a pick or my thumb. I don't ever boost the top end much. Sometimes I'll boost the lows at 40-50Hz or 100Hz. It depends where the bass needs help.

EQ can help a little, but you need to start with technique and a good-sounding bass. You can also get carried away with trying to make everything clean and pristine. I like to mike an amp in the studio; I've got Ampeg B-12 and B-18 amps I use for a vintage sound, and they take it back to a more soulful place. They sound good when you turn them up—they get a little nasty.

■ *How much do you think about note length?*

That's just another part of the vocabulary. It's wrong to have one sound or style, because every song is different. Sometimes I make sure my note is gone by the time the snare drum is hit, and sometimes I let the notes ring throughout the song.

When I use a pick I usually lay my palm down on the string and strike it at the same time I pick. The pick gives a great top-end click and the palm adds an enormous low end. There are misfires, but when that technique works it's an amazing sound.

I don't try to project my style onto anybody else. I try to do what's right for the particular moment. You have to be aware of the length of each note, the tone, your volume in relation to the other instruments, and if you're playing too much.

■ *Has the ability to double helped your career?*

It has helped so much! There's no telling how many dates I've gotten because I could play string bass and electric bass. Playing the string bass has become one of my most passionate musical pursuits in the past few years. I've spent a lot of time working on technique and trying to expand what I can do. I'm playing a lot more jazz now, tailoring my technique to get the sounds of my favorite records.

I'm kind of an educated hack on upright—my technique is a blend of hillbilly bass and the classical technique I studied in college. But the technique has to serve the sound you're trying to get. I know a number of tremendous rockabilly and bluegrass bassists who don't have particularly good technique, but they can get the sound that's right for their music.

■ *What strings are you using on your uprights?*

On one bass I use gut on the *D* and *G* and steel Thomastik Spirocores on the *E* and *A*. The other bass I record with is all Spirocores.

■ *In Nashville is it important to be easy to work with?*

It's essential. Nashville's talent pool is vast. There's no reason to put up with a prima donna, someone who has a bad attitude, or someone who shows up drunk or unable to perform. If you can't make the artist and other players feel comfortable and glad to have you on the session, then they won't perform their best. You've got to be a diplomat as well as a player, and sometimes you have to be a cheerleader and help someone out of a slump.

■ *Any other advice for the next generation of studio bassists?*

Arm yourself with as many skills as you can. Expose yourself to as many styles of music as possible. Learn to read music. You have to be prepared to handle anything that's thrown at you. Versatility is the key.

Track 11

Chuck Berry Style

In the style of Glenn Worf

Courtesy Of Glenn Worf
Used By Permission

Bob
Wray

"Why not go for things? The producer will let you know if you've gone too far, and it's easy to pull back."

Selected Discography

With B. B. King: *Love Me Tender*, MCA. With Ray Charles: *Friends*, CBS. With Mac Davis: *Baby Don't Get Hooked on Me*, Columbia. With Hank Williams Jr.: *Family Tradition*, Warner Bros. With Ronnie Milsap: *True Believer*, Liberty. With George Jones: *I Am What I Am*, Epic. With Kathy Mattea: *Willow in the Wind*, Mercury. With Tanya Tucker: *Greatest Hits*, Capitol. With Emmylou Harris: *Brand New Dance*, Reprise. With Mark Chesnutt: *Longnecks & Short Stories*, *Almost Goodbye*, MCA.

Biography

Former Muscle Shoals studio hand Bob Wray has played on scores of hit records throughout the years. Now based in Nashville, Bob has continued to be a first-call bassist because of his ability to adapt to current

musical trends. Bob's extensive credit list includes hits by Ray Charles, Al Green, Willie Nelson, Mac Davis, Hank Williams Jr., Ronnie Milsap, and Joe Cocker.

■ *How did you get started playing bass?*

I come from a musical family. My mother, who is 80 years old, is still playing church organ. After years of trying to learn the piano, I switched to trumpet. That didn't work out, so I switched to upright bass. I played it in the orchestra starting in junior high. In my junior year of high school I got an electric bass and started playing in bands.

I learned how to read when I was real young, but the problem was if my mother played a melody, I'd play the melody, too. But we discovered I played by ear very well. That's been good for studio work, because I don't do much sight-reading on most sessions.

■ *You like to explore lines that use the whole bass.*

I don't think the bass should be limited to just the foundation, although sometimes you have to do it that way. I remember years ago I would sit down with a 4-string bass and learn a simple song with chordal movements and melodies just to see what it sounded like. In sessions I'm often asked to play melodic bass lines, and I've played little countermelodies on a lot of records over the years. It's basically the producer's call. Five- and 6-string basses are a lot of fun for that kind of playing because you have more room to stretch out.

■ *Do you think your melodic sense and your willingness to try new things has sustained your career?*

I think so. When I first started playing, I always took it as a compliment when I was called down for overplaying, especially when they said, "It's a little too much, but I like the direction you're going." Why not go for things? The producer will let you know if you've gone too far, and it's easy to pull back.

■ *Do you mind suggestions made by the producer?*

Not at all, because that's what he's there for. There are people who call themselves producers who never say a word in their sessions, and they end up being produced by the players. But I've

worked for some wonderful producers who hire a good band and expect you to come up with things, but will suggest parts, too.

On Mark Chesnutt's single "Old Flames" there was a breakdown in the song I had no intention of playing because bass is not considered a solo instrument in country music. But the producer asked me to play a solo there, so I played a double-finger [thumb and first finger] descending line for four bars, and the producer loved it. It ended up being a hit record, and I've gotten a lot of compliments on it.

■ *What was your first session?*

It was with Travis Wammack, who had an instrumental hit in the mid '60s called "Scratchy." I was on tour with him, and he got me started doing session work. We recorded at Hi Recording in Memphis—I think the tune was an instrumental version of "Fire" by Jimi Hendrix.

Next I recorded with a horn player named Ace Cannon, which was quite an experience. Ace walked into the studio with a .45-caliber pistol, a couple of cans of beer, and some pills, and he said, "Let's cut." I was 21 at the time. Travis called me a while later and told me I should go to Muscle Shoals because there was an opening there. I went down and auditioned for Rick Hall, who was a producer and owner of Fame Studios; the audition ended up being a session for Bobby Hatfield of the Righteous Brothers. Then I did some tracks for Hall with Willie Hightower, who was an R&B singer. That was really the audition. They called a week later and said I had the job, so I moved to Muscle Shoals in 1970, when I was 23.

■ *What was working at Fame like?*

Rick Hall was also a bass player, and rule No. 1 was that you played his bass through his amp with an old RCA tube mike on it. It was a '57 P-Bass with medium-high action and flatwounds that were never changed; the amp was an old Fender Bassman head with a 12-inch speaker. They put the mike eight to twelve inches from the cabinet and didn't use a direct box. It was an 8-track format with the bass drum and the bass guitar on the same track. Later on Rick let me play my 1960 Jazz Bass, even though he didn't like two-pickup basses. His bass is now on loan to the Rock and Roll Hall of Fame.

Rick's theory was the harder you played, the better the bass sounded; it produced a minute amount of distortion that gave the tone the funkiness he was looking for. Since I played hard I put Vaseline on my two picking fingers to keep my calluses from clicking on the strings. It also helped keep my fingers from getting sore, since we did six-hour sessions and would sometimes spend the whole time on one song. There was a bass booth where I sat when tracking, and I'd wipe off the excess Vaseline on the burlap walls. We used the Number System, but most of the time nothing was written out. Rick would sometimes hum the part to you.

When I first started playing at Fame, Rick had just produced the song "Patches" for Clarence Carter. I finished the album, which became a major hit.

Things really started rolling then; in 1971 Rick was named Producer of the Year.

When Rick believed a song was a hit and wanted it cut a certain way, it didn't matter how long it took to get it right. When Mac Davis cut "Baby Don't Get Hooked on Me" it took us two days to get the track.

It was sometimes tough working for Rick, and if you couldn't cut it he would have someone else lined up. I've been at sessions where he had two or three bass players in case you couldn't get the track. He was real critical about the bass, but if there was ever a school for session bass players, that was it.

■ *Who was tracking at your rival, Muscle Shoals Sound Studios?*

David Hood was working at Muscle Shoals; he played on some of the Aretha Franklin records, though Tommy Cogbill did most of them in Memphis at American Studios. There was some competition between the studios, and both were doing very well.

■ *Why did you move to Atlanta in 1973?*

I had gotten burned out on Muscle Shoals, because there was no place to play live and it was a dry county. Some of the guys at Fame moved to Atlanta to be the studio band for a publisher named Bill Lowry. I did a record there with Sammie Joe called "Tell Me a Lie" that did pretty well, and I also worked with Billy Joe Royal and the Tams.

I cut some gospel records in Chattanooga, but they weren't the quality of the Muscle Shoals projects. In 1976 keyboardist/producer Barry Beckett called me to work with the Muscle Shoals Horns, who had gotten a record deal. We cut three albums of real funky dance music.

Some Nashville producers started cutting in Muscle Shoals. Buddy Killen brought in Diana Trask and Joe Tex, and Billy Sherrill brought artists like Janie Fricke. I recorded Hank Williams Jr.'s "Family Tradition" in Muscle Shoals, playing a Jazz Bass with my sweater hanging across the strings and using my thumb.

I met a lot of Nashville people during those sessions, and I made my move in 1980. My first Nashville sessions were with Sherrill—we cut a record with, of all people, Chuck Woolery, who was host of the *Love Connection* TV show. It was a "Tribute to America" kind of thing. I worked for Billy for ten years. We cut records with George Jones, David Allan Coe, Lacy J. Dalton, Johnny Rodriguez, Ray Charles, Willie Nelson, Mickey Gilley, and lots of others. Buddy Killen used me on T. G. Sheppard's "I Loved 'Em Every One" and "Finally."

■ *Did you bring that Muscle Shoals feel with you to Nashville?*

I've been told that; when people want something funky they ask for my Muscle Shoals feel. Muscle Shoals gave me a lot; some of the biggest records I ever played on came from there. My first major record other than the *Patches* album was "One Bad Apple" by the Osmond Brothers. I only had a few months' recording experience when that track came along, and it sold five million copies. I was excited to hear

myself on the radio, sometimes two or three times an hour.

That recording is an example of how putting space between notes lets the track breathe and keeps the funk alive. Drummer Larrie Londin told me "One Bad Apple" was one of his all-time favorite records.

■ *How did you hook up with Ronnie Milsap?*

I played on the demo of "Lost in the Fifties Tonight," and when Ronnie heard it he wanted the same players on the record. I had been trying to get his account for years. I played on that session and ended up playing on his records for the next ten years.

I introduced Ronnie to the 5-string bass. I used to sit right next to him while he played piano on his tracks, and I remember playing the low *B* string and him kind of flinching and saying, "What is that?" But he liked the 5-string, though on more traditional songs he would tell me to play it like a 4-string, so I knew not to get below the low *E*.

■ *What's your main bass?*

A Pedulla 5-string with EMG PJ pickups and preamp; I like having onboard EQ so I can change the tone if I need to. I've been playing 5-strings for 12 years, and I use the Pedulla on most of my sessions. I also use a Tobias 6-string, and once in a while I play a Washburn 5-string acoustic bass, miking it and running a DI to the board; it's an interesting sound. Sometimes I use a Modulus fretless 5-string to overdub melodic lines over fretted tracks. I've also got a couple of Music Man basses. My strings are D'Addario Slowounds and DRs gauged .45-.125 or .128; I switch between stainless-steel and nickel depending on the project. I change strings every two weeks or so, also depending on the project. I'm not afraid to go in with live-sounding new strings, because sometimes they keep the bass from getting lost in a track.

■ *When a couple of acoustic guitars are creating a lot of rumble on a track, what can you do to help the bass cut through?*

If an acoustic guitar has a string ringing out, it can play havoc with the bass. I've been accused more than once of making a mistake or having a bad-sounding bass because of an improperly recorded acoustic guitar. But when they

isolated the acoustic they heard the overtones that were ringing and clashing with the bass. One thing you can try is boost the bass a little at 600–900Hz. I use a Pultec broad-band tube EQ that lets you choose an available frequency and lock into that.

■ *Do you ever have problems using your rack system?*

It becomes a problem when engineers add their EQ to yours; if they make the bass sound totally different from your own EQ it makes it hard to play. Most engineers end up deciding I have all I need in my rack, and they'll tell me as I track what they need. In the control room the engineer is getting a different perspective through the monitor speakers. I'm judging the sound by what I hear in the phones. I run through a Mor Me box, so I can hear what my own EQ is.

■ *What has the business taught you over the years?*

I've learned a lot of discipline. There are a lot of sessions that are fun, and there are some that aren't. But I thoroughly enjoy making records and I've never really gotten tired of it; the variety has kept me going. I think if you have the opportunity to play, then play, because you might be able to do this for a living like I have. It's very gratifying to look back and see the list of artists, movies, and albums I've played on.

**Track
12**

In the style of Bob Wray

Courtesy Of Bob Wray
Used By Permission

Remembering Roy Huskey Jr.

"Sometimes I'll leave a little sloppiness in a track if it seems to project the right feeling."

Selected Discography

With Nanci Griffith: *Once in a Very Blue Moon*, Philo. With Ricky Van Shelton: *Wild-Eyed Dream*, Columbia. With the Judds: *River of Time*, RCA. With Mark O'Connor, *Heroes*, Warner Bros. With Emmylou Harris: *At the Ryman*, *Brand New Dance*, Reprise. With Alan Jackson, *Here in the Real World*, Arista. With Garth Brooks: *Limited Series*, Capitol. With Steve Earle: *El Corazon*, Warner Bros. With George Jones, *I Lived to Tell It All*, MCA.

Biography

Chances are when just about anyone plays traditional country upright, they think of Roy Huskey Jr. Roy, who died of cancer in September 1997 at age 40, was *the* first-call upright bassist in Nashville country sessions and one of the top bluegrass session players. But apart from his toneful, tasty, in-the-pocket bass work, Roy will be remembered for his modesty, generosity, and humor. His

recorded work spans artists including Linda Ronstadt, Garth Brooks, Alan Jackson, Ricky Van Shelton, George Jones, and Emmylou Harris. Roy gave this interview in the year before his death.

■ *How did you get started on the bass?*

Initially I played along with records and listened to what other bass players were doing. I started on upright.

■ *Were there any particular bassists you checked out?*

It was a couple of years before I started paying attention to other players. Back then I didn't know who I was listening to because most of the records didn't list the players. Of course whenever I could find out, it was great. I got to where I could tell the difference between the different bass players, especially the local players like Bob Moore, Billy Linneman, Henry Strzelecki, and my dad, Junior Huskey. [*These bassists played upright and some electric on most of the country records that came out of Nashville from 1950 through the 1970s.*] I also liked Ray Brown, who played on the *Merv Griffin Show*, and Dalton Dillingham. Dalton came to Nashville from L.A. and stayed a few years. He had a completely different approach and was one of the first bassists I ever heard using Thomastik strings. He worked with Benny Goodman at one time. I checked out Willie Dixon, too; I'm really into the blues.

■ *What kind of music were you listening to at the time?*

All kinds. I would listen to whatever came along. I made no exceptions and would try to learn a little of everything.

■ *Did your dad offer advice when you were getting started?*

Not a lot, because he was so busy playing on sessions. He knew I was playing and had heard me a little bit, and that was the extent of it. It was not that he meant not to be there; it was because he was working so much and

was not able to be very involved. He didn't pressure me to play.

■ *It's been said you play like your father.*

On certain things our styles are pretty close. I've listened to his playing a lot over the years. My dad died a few years after I started playing, so his influence came mostly later on when I began listening to the records he played on.

■ *What was your first upright?*

It was one of my dad's old basses, which I still have. It's a plywood Gretsch that looks kind of like a Kay. The veneer pattern is a little bit deeper than a Kay's, particularly on the sides and back. It doesn't look like a plywood instrument. I would guess it was made in the 1940s. It had some old gut strings on it when I started playing it.

■ *What was your first pro job?*

It was with Del Wood—she was a ragtime piano player. She invited me to play with her on the Grand Ole Opry, and it was a lot of fun. I worked with her for about 10 years after that. She did some road work, too.

I was 16 when I first started doing session work. I was doing some recording during my years with Del, and I did demos and projects with other players. I knew early on that I wanted to do sessions.

■ *Did you have a hard time adjusting to the recording environment?*

Not really. By then I had paid enough attention to what other bass players were doing, and I had a pretty good handle on it.

■ *When you were coming up through the ranks, what players were doing most of the sessions?*

Bob Moore and Henry Strzelecki were doing the bulk of the work, and Billy Linneman was really starting to take off. Billy was good friends with my dad.

■ *You were a young player who got to rub elbows with the giants of country session bass. Did they ever give you pointers?*

I mostly just watched them very carefully and picked it up on my own. I used to really like to watch Bob Moore. He had a knack for making it look so easy. Billy Linneman is very precise on the instrument and looks highly trained.

■ *Tell me about your dad's recording work.*

It's hard to know where to start. He did most of the early Tammy Wynette records and records for Freddie Hart, Sonny James, George Jones, Loretta Lynn, and many others.

■ *You use both gut and metal strings on your different basses. How do you decide which to use?*

When I get a new bass I try different strings and let the bass dictate what type will work best.

■ *What brand of strings do you use?*

For gut strings I've mostly used LaBellas. I'm not sure if this is true or not, but I heard they started using goat gut instead of sheep gut in the later years. I think the change affected the quality a little bit, and now they're a lit-

tle more temperamental. For steel strings I use Thomastik Spirocore Weich gauge. The Orchestra-gauge set has a more complex sound but doesn't quite have the balance for my taste. They also seem to have more hot spots. Some instruments react differently, though, so be your own judge. To amplify my bass I use an Underwood pickup.

■ *Do you use sets that have metal-wound gut on the E and A strings with plain gut on the D and G?*

Yes, the LaBellas. The metal-wound *E* and *A* have a little more sustain and volume and a more versatile tone than plain gut, but it doesn't always work out that way. Some players use gut for the *D* and *G* with all-metal *E* and *A* strings. The metal wound gut can loosen sometimes, but the last few sets I've used haven't had that problem.

■ *Who works on your basses?*

I do all my own setups. I'll take wood off the fingerboard if the instrument needs leveling, and I'll pull a neck off if I need to, but sometimes I have to get outside help—I've gotten in trouble a couple of times when I bit off more than I could chew! Bill Dibb has done some work for me in the past. He's actually a guitar maker and he does good work.

■ *How do you determine your soundpost location?*

Trial and error, listening, VU meters, anything I can think of to get it right.

■ *What do you do when a bass has a weak-sounding E string?*

That's a problem with a lot of basses, particularly plywood instruments. Sometimes they don't really speak out, and there isn't much you can do with them.

■ *How do you like your action?*

It depends, but for the most part my preference is to set the action low for steel strings. But I've played a few steel-string basses with high action, and they sounded great. Playing with high action can be rough on you, though, especially with steel strings. Most of my gut-string basses have pretty high action. I generally keep the nut action pretty low, as low as I can go without rattles. Lower nut action makes it easier to play, just like low bridge action does.

■ *What do you practice?*

I try to find new techniques. For instance, I have one that involves a hand spread that allows me to do a lot of things with my left hand—I have my hand stretched from the $B\flat$ to the $C\sharp$ on the A string. I like to develop hand positioning for easy access to notes.

■ *How much electric bass do you play?*

Very little [*laughs*], though I've played off and on for years. When I do a session on electric I let the engineer take care of the sound. I don't use a rack. I play a Modulus 5-string, an old Ampeg 4-string electric bass, and a '59 Fender Jazz Bass with really old strings on it. I rarely use that bass anymore.

■ *Do you have a mike preference for recording your upright?*

I own an RCA 44 ribbon mike. It has a low-end that sounds compressed; on certain things it works really well. But usually I let the engineer use what he wants to use. It always comes out a little different that way, and that might make me play or think differently. I like to record without headphones when I get the chance, especially when there are other acoustic instruments in the room. I also don't use a tuner with my upright; I check my tuning with the piano.

■ *Do you play hard when you're tracking?*

It depends on what's happening with the engineer, the band, and everything else. Mikes, EQ, and compression make a difference, too. Sometimes I barely hit the string, yet it yields a big sound in the track. Then in some situations you can't play hard enough. The environment dictates what you need to do.

■ *Do producers usually let you play what you want?*

For the most part, yes. Sometimes they'll choose what they want played, like a certain style or line. I'm not a strong reader, but if I get into situations where I'm reading all the time, I get better quickly. If I don't read for a long time, I get rusty. I read just enough to get myself in trouble!

■ *What are some of your slapping techniques?*

There are a couple of different styles I do. For rockabilly I use three fingers to pull the string. For bluegrass I'll use only one finger. I usually pop or pull the string and then come back and slap the board. You have to do it a lot for

your hands to get used to it. Generally I'll use gut for slapping, but I've also used metal strings. If the engineer is getting a good sound on the bass, it can be a lot of fun to slap on metal strings. They have a more raucous sound, and you get a lot more overtones. I show up with a gut-string bass for most recordings. I have shown up with two basses—a gut and a steel string—but not very often. I'm only able to do it because I have a '71 Fleetwood Cadillac!

■ *Have you done much touring with the string bass?*

Not a lot of touring that required flying, but I have toured with a string bass—for instance, with Emmylou Harris. We toured all over the country in a bus with the bass in an equipment truck that followed us from job to job. The techs were very good at handling the gear and transporting it safely. I never had any problems to speak of. I usually bring my old briefcase, which contains a soundpost setter, extra strings, tools, and sandpaper for changing the action if needed.

■ *For many years you've been one of the first-call bassists in Nashville. What advice can you offer the aspiring string bassist who wants to be a session player?*

Oh, Lord! [*Laughs.*] All I can say is hang in there. You just have to keep at it to make it in Nashville. I've been lucky to be able to see and hear the great players up close, and to pick up something from each one.

I've had work and encouragement given to me from almost all of the players around town. John Hartford really hung in there with me when times got tough, and there were also Benny Martin, Jimmy Martin, Roy Acuff, Bud Wendell at the Opry, and, of course, Del Wood. I owe so many people so much.

Donations to help Roy's family may be made to the Roy Huskey Jr. Fund, c/o NationsBank of Tennessee Private Client Group, 7th Floor, 1 NationsBank Plaza, Nashville, TN 37239; attn: Deborah Roto.

Styles You Need to Know

- Blues
- Rock
- Country
- Latin
- Jazz

Track 13

Blues
Tribute To Tommy Shannon

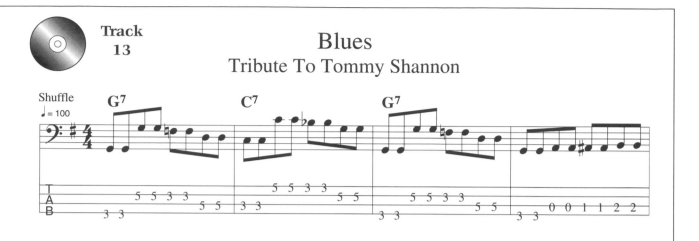

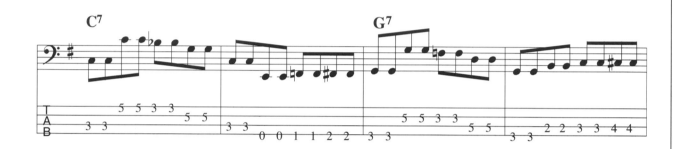

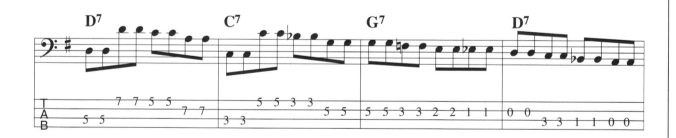

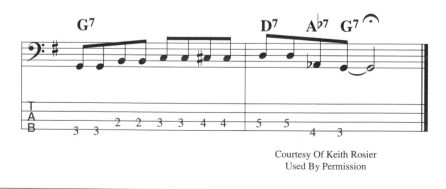

Courtesy Of Keith Rosier
Used By Permission

Track
15

Country
Tribute To Roy Huskey Jr.

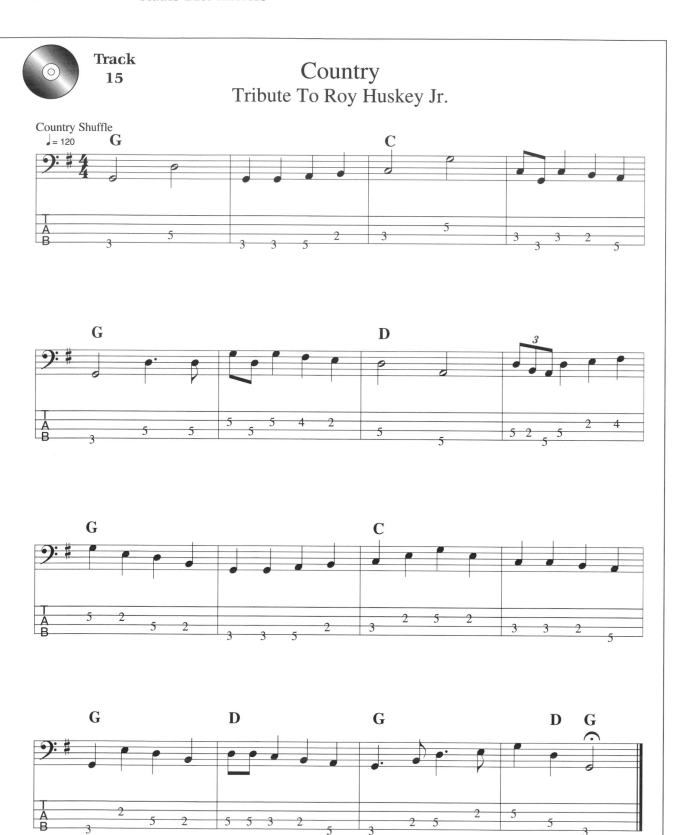

Courtesy Of Keith Rosier
Used By Permission

Track 16

Latin
Tribute To Lightnin' Chance

Track 17

Jazz
Tribute To Ray Brown

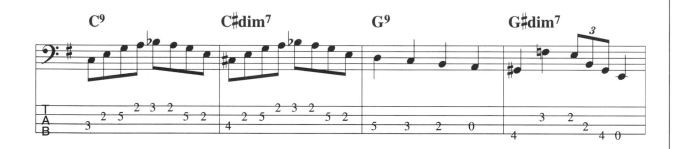

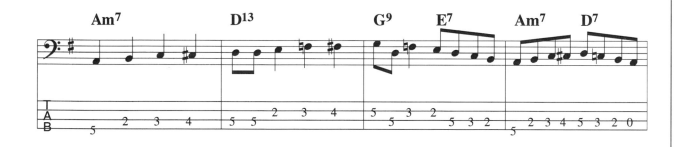

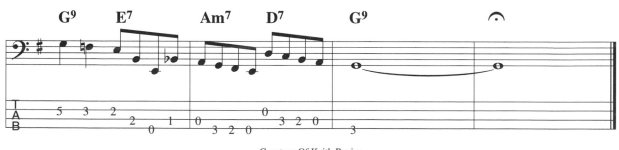

Courtesy Of Keith Rosier
Used By Permission

About the Author

Keith Rosiér has played bass professionally for 20 years. Raised in Texas, he moved to Los Angeles in 1979, at age 19 to pursue a music career. He has worked with Joe Houston, Vince Gill, Kathy Mathis, Charlie Sexton, Steve Earle, Junior Watson, Lacy J. Dalton, Johnny Lee, and others. His movie score and soundtrack credits includes *Beverly Hills Cop II, Exposed, Return to Two Moon Junction, California,* and *The Effects of Magic.* As an author he has published two other books *Jump 'N' Blues Bass,* and *The Lost Art of Country Bass.* He is currently working on his fourth book titled, *Father To Be.* Keith, his wife, Denise, and daughter, Madeleine live in the Los Angeles area.

Keith can be contacted at DRosier@aol.com.

Photo Credits

Don Was—Page vii, photo courtesy Don Was archives

Pete Anderson—Page 17, photo courtesy Anderson archives

Dusty Wakeman—Page 21, photo courtesy Wakeman archives

Mike Brignardello—Pages 30 & 35, photos courtesy Rebecca A. Walk

Mike Chapman—Pages 37 & 41, photos courtesy Mike Chapman archives

Nathan East—Page 43, photo courtesy Tatsuo Kusumoto; page 46, photo courtesy Nathan East

Hutch Hutchinson—Page 50, photo courtesy Don Was; page 54, photo courtesy H. Hutchinson

Roy Huskey Jr.—Pages 102 & 106, photos by Rick Malkin

Bob Moore—Pages 56 & 62, photos courtesy Moore archives

Larry Paxton—Pages 64 & 68, photos courtesy Paxton archives

Dave Pomeroy—Pages 70 & 74, photos courtesy Pomeroy archives

Leland Sklar—Page 76, photo courtesy Richard Newman; page82, photo courtesy Sklar archives

Neil Stubenhaus—Page 84, photo courtesy Dee Dee Hart; page 88, photo courtesy Alison Stubenhaus

Glenn Worf—Pages 90 & 94, photos courtesy Worf archives

Bob Wray—Pages 96 & 100, photos courtesy Wray archives

CD Recording Credits

Players:
- Ron Finn: Guitars
- Doug Livingston: Keys, Steel Guitar
- John Molo: Drums, Percussion
- Keith Rosiér: Electric Bass, Upright Bass
- Ian Miller: Recording, Mixing

Basses and related gear used for the CD recording:

- John Carruthers 4 string electric bass with d-tuner, EMG PJ pickups, new LaBella Hard Rockin' Steel strings (45-110 gauge) and Demeter onboard pre-amp (low end slightly boosted); this bass used on track(s) 3, 4, 7, 8, 9, 10, 14.

- Epiphone Jack Casady Signature electric bass with new LaBella Flatwound strings (45-105 gauge) and a little piece of foam placed in front of the bridge saddles; this bass was used on track(s) 2, 5, 11, 12, 13.

- 1920 German 3/4 size carved double bass (upright bass) with Pirastro Flat-Chromesteel G, D, and A strings with Spiro Core weich gauge (light gauge) E string. The pickup on the bass, a David Gage model, was connected to the board having its own track. Also used was an AKG 414 mike placed 6 inches directly in front of the bass bridge, recorded on a separate track, too. When mixed, the mike was favored, and compressed slightly with a tube unit; this bass was used on track(s) 6, 15, 16, and 17.

All basses, including the David Gage upright pickup were run through a Glocken-klang Heart Core bass head with EQ engaged, and boosting (+2 or 3 dB) at 60Hz, 130Hz, 4.2KHz, and 12KHz. The Heart Core DI was connected to a tube compressor, using minimal compression. The output of the compressor was then connected to a Soundcraft studio console (board), using one of the console's onboard mike preamps, then routed to a Tascam DA-88 digital recorder, and recorded on its own track. The effect sends (2) of the Heart Core were sent to a Fender Bassman vintage tube amp modified to allow the amp to be disconnected from a speaker source (without burning up the amp—see your amp tech for this "mod") and a preamp line out added, too; this amp's output was connected to a console mike pre-amp and recorded on its own track.

The remaining effect send of the Glock was sent to a Boss Bass Chorus pedal with its output sent to a console mike pre and recorded on its own track, too. The Glock track is 85% of the sound heard on the CD, and I compressed it again slightly with a tube unit when mixing—with the Bassman and chorus tracks used slightly for distortion and color. The phase of the Bassman track had to be adjusted by the engineer so it could be blended with the Glock track. I added very little EQ when mixing (on any instrument), and any distortion heard is intentional.

• Additional Recording: Dangerous Waters Music Recording Studio, Ron Finn, Engineer, West Los Angeles, CA.

• CD Mastering: Evatone, 1-800-EVA-TONE

• Jesse Gress: Music/Tab Editor

Note: If your stereo doesn't have a balance control, you can try disconnecting your system's right and left speaker, depending on what you want to hear. Caution: Be careful when disconnecting a speaker cord and be sure the speaker cord wires never touch, if they do, it could damage your stereo or amp.

Note: To practice recording, record the right channel music of the CD onto a two or more channel recorder (a Tascam Porta-Studio, for instance—a cassette deck will not work in this instance, unless you can turn off the record mode on the track with the CD music). A two-track reel-to-reel can work, too. After recording the CD's right channel music onto the recorder, be sure not to record over it. Then record your own bassline along with the CD's right channel that you just recorded.

What's On the CD:

1. Tuning track, 2. In the style of Mike Brignardello, 3. In the style of Mike Chapman, 4. In the style of Nathan East, 5. In the style of Hutch Hutchinson, 6. In the style of Bob Moore, 7. In the style of Larry Paxton, 8. In the style of Dave Pomeroy, 9. In the style of Leland Sklar, 10. In the style of Neil Stubenhaus, 11. In the style of Glenn Worf, 12. In the style of Bob Wray, 13. Blues, 14. Rock , 15. Country, 16. Latin, 17. Jazz

To hear bass only: pan left
To hear band only: pan right
To hear both: pan center

Special thanks to LaBella Bass Strings: The official string of *Studio Bass Masters*.